Party Piece

A comedy

Richard Harris

Suggested by the author's
earlier play, *Local Affairs*

Samuel French – London
New York – Toronto – Hollywood

PARTY PIECE

This revised version of the play was first performed on April 11th, by the Horseshoe Theatre Company, Basingstoke. The cast was as follows:

Michael Smethurst	Guy Siner
Mrs Hinson	Maria Charles
Roma Smethurst	Charlotte Attenborough
David Hinson	David McAlister
Jennifer Hinson	Joanna Van Gyseghem
Toby Hancock	Graham Sinclair
Sandy Lloyd-Meredith	Lynn Clayton
Director	Adrian Reynolds
Designer	Elroy Ashmore

CHARACTERS

Michael Smethurst
Roma Smethurst, his wife
Mrs Hinson
David, her son
Jennifer, her daughter-in-law
Toby
Sandy

The action takes place in the gardens of the Smethursts
and the Hinsons

Time—the present

Plays by Richard Harris also published by Samuel French Ltd

Albert
Is It Something I Said?
Keeping Mum
Local Affairs
The Maintenance Man
Outside Edge
Partners
Stepping Out
Visiting Hour

ACT I

The gardens of a pair of terraced Victorian houses in West London. A Saturday afternoon in summer

The rear elevation of the houses shows them to be a mirror-image of each other and identical in structure. Each has, on opposite sides, an extension at right angles to the main structure containing the kitchens, with the bathrooms above, which have frosted windows. Each house has a pair of french windows

The Hinson house L is in its original state, looked after but not 'improved'. There is a lawn and flowerbeds. There are random little piles of plant pots, a plastic bucket and a garden fork. DS, a small pond fashioned from a butler sink sunk into the grass. DL of the extension, there is a crumbling old jerry-built shed. A washing-line runs from the shed to the DS end of the left-hand wooden garden fence. On the grass, angled towards the sun, there is a nineteen thirties dining chair and an old bamboo table on which is a copy of the "TV Times". Parked outside the part-open kitchen door is a Zimmer walking frame with a basket attached

The Smethurst house is the end of the terrace and has been extensively improved. All the windows have been double-glazed, while all the exterior pipework and guttering has been renewed in plastic. What can be seen of the roof shows it to be re-tiled. The back of the house has been trellised and new creepers are trained up it. There are colourful windowboxes on the upper windowsills. The garden is extremely neat, totally paved, with the occasional bed of new shrub, each of them conspicuously labelled. Old chimney pots contain trailing plants. DR of the extension there is a new and rather small shed, the door of which is UR, unseen. DS there is a rotary washing line. A pair of hinged trestles and two table tops of different design and dimension lean against the shed

The fence dividing the two houses exists unseen and imagined, but very much in evidence

When the CURTAIN *rises, the stage is empty but from behind the Smethurst shed, Michael can be heard cursing to himself as he moves things around. He appears from behind the shed, carrying a pair of trestles which he sets down with the others*

Michael Smethurst is in his mid-thirties and is extremely neat, diet-lean, seldom still and takes himself very seriously. His moustache was grown years ago to make him look older. He wears an immaculate tracksuit and a pair of trainer shoes

He shakes and sucks the finger he has just caught in the shed door as he surveys the garden for a moment, then moves to peer briefly over the fence. He frowns, holding the frown as his gaze falls on to one of his shrubs. He walks over to it, examines a leaf and then takes out a tissue to gently wipe the leaf

Michael (*somewhat self-consciously*) That's better, eh? How are you settling in? Everything all right for you, is it? Good—good. (*He runs out of things to say*) I'll—umm—I'll let you get on then. Well done.

Michael exits behind the shed as:

Mrs Hinson comes out of her kitchen with a pile of washing which she drapes in the Zimmer basket. She puts her handbag on the table and uses the frame to move across to the washing line

She is a working-class widow in her late sixties. Her mind is a mixture of pure gristle and animal cunning. She feigns deafness when it suits. She dresses top to toe in clothes from Marks and Spencers and is wearing a floral pinny and slippers. She seldom goes anywhere without her handbag over her arm, even at home. She moves perfectly well without the use of the walking frame

She takes a damp cloth from her pinny and runs it along the washing line wiping it clean as:

Roma appears in the Smethurst kitchen doorway. She is short and has a slight weight problem. She wears a headband and a tracksuit and trainers that exactly match those worn by Michael. She is loaded down with shopping bags which include ten french sticks, and a large bag of barbecue charcoal

Roma Mickey?
Michael (*off*) Hello.
Roma I'm back. (*She puts the charcoal on the step*)

Roma exits carrying the rest of the bags back inside the kitchen as:

Michael enters from behind the shed:

Michael Any problems?

Roma enters the garden

Roma Quite the reverse actually.
Michael Ah, you got the charcoal, well done. (*He puts the charcoal behind the shed*)

During the following speech Roma stands on tiptoe on the french window step to look over the fence

Mrs Hinson is pegging out her washing which consists of dusters, tea towels, a pinafore and underwear

Roma frowns slightly but doesn't waver in the recounting of the story

Roma They were rather quiet in the car and I thought—well—I know we've talked it through with them but—first time they've been away on their own—stand by for a last minute little tizzy—William if not James——

instead of which, as soon as I stop the car it's, "Off you go mummy have a lovely party, see you on Sunday." Honestly.

Michael Just as we thought then—weekend with grandma—they'll love it.

Roma And so will she. Honestly Mickey, you should have seen her. I just know she'll have been out buying all the wrong things. "Please remember, Mummy", I said, "No sweets, definitely no orange cordial and possibly one hour's telly", and fat chance of that I shouldn't wonder. I'll make you a little sarnie, shall I?

Roma exits into the kitchen

Michael Roma.

Roma puts her head out the door, knowing what is coming

I don't need a sandwich thank you and neither do you.

There is nothing heavy in the following exchange. Michael teasing Roma about her weight is one of their 'fun things'

Roma (*indicating*) Just a tiny . . .

Michael No nibbling between meals.

Roma (*indicating a smaller size*) Just——

Michael No nibbling.

Roma Oh it's all right for you, you never put on——

Michael All right, eat what you want, Fattie.

Roma Meanie. Oh you've got the tables out—well *done*. (*She moves to look at them admiringly*)

Michael What d'you think?

Roma Excellent, Mickey.

Michael Worth the effort?

Roma Oh they are, they're smashing.

Michael The things people—(*miming*) throw away.

Roma I know, I know . . .

During the following Roma moves busily in and out of the kitchen

Michael sets about the apparently none-too-easy task of taking down the rotary line

I took your short cut through Stanley Crescent, which is smashing by the way, *much* shorter, then I went via Gladstone Avenue which has two more "For Sales" up. What I think is really smashing, Mike, is the way the whole area is coming up. You were absolutely right of course. I mean *I* thought Gladstone Avenue, for example, was a lost cause but it's really on the move. Another couple of years and it could be really villagy.

The Hinson doorbell rings

Mrs Hinson does not respond

Michael Oh yes, Nick phoned. They're not coming.

Roma Oh, that's sad.

Michael They've had to go down and see her parents in Crawley or somewhere.
Roma Reigate.
Michael Sure he said Crawley.
Roma No, Reigate. I remember Gilly saying her parents live in Reigate.

The Hinson doorbell rings

(*Lowering her voice*) Have you mentioned it to next door by the way?
Michael I did knock. No answer.
Roma Actually—(*tiptoeing to look*) she's in the garden.
Michael Have a word then.
Roma I'd rather you did it, Mike. It's about time you introduced yourself to her anyway. (*She enunciates carefully*) Mrs Hinson.
Michael Roma. Simple—communication.
Roma I remember the last time I tried to communicate.
Michael All the more reason to plant the flag. (*He gets on with taking down the rotary line*)

Roma goes to the fence and tries to look over but it is too high for her

Roma exits into the kitchen as:

David comes out of the Hinson french windows. He is in his early forties. He is big, heavily-built, ambling and seemingly placid. He wears good cashmere and a good watch, carries a mobile telephone. He stands for a moment, watching his mother pegging out her washing

David (*moving over to her*) Hello Mum.
Mrs Hinson (*jumping*) What you do that for?
David Why don't you answer the door?
Mrs Hinson Creeping up on your own mother like that.
David You don't answer the door.
Mrs Hinson You've got a key, haven't you?
David Just as well—don't I get a kiss?

Mrs Hinson tilts her head and he kisses her brow. Kissing does not come easy in this family and she pushes him away indicating her handbag which she has put on the bamboo table

Mrs Hinson Pass me my bag, will you?

David gives her the handbag as she lowers herself into the chair

Creeping up on me like that, you've brought on one of my heads. (*She almost snatches the bag from him and delves into it for her pills as:*)

Roma enters with a pair of aluminium kitchen steps which she sets up near the fence and climbs on them. She is about to call to Mrs Hinson when;

David I'll fetch you some water. (*He puts down the mobile phone*)

David exits into the kitchen

On seeing him, Roma ducks down out of sight and gets off the steps

.

Roma (*in a lowered voice*) There's someone with her.

Michael *I'll* do it, softie.

Roma No, honestly, Mike, there's someone with her. If you do speak, I wonder if it might be an idea to say something about the washing?

Roma exits with the steps as:

David enters with a glass of water which he gives to his mother

David I see you've been polishing the step again.

Michael exits

Mrs Hinson You're not saying there's anything wrong with polishing my step, are you?

David Apart from the fact I nearly broke my neck.

She swallows down a pill, making much of it as:

I don't like you cleaning the step. I don't like seeing you on your hands and knees, I never have.

Mrs Hinson You don't see me on my hands and knees, you're never here.

David (*wandering across to look through the shed window*) Yeah, I know I'm very naughty and I've been meaning to come over but the fact of the matter is I met this fella who said how would you like to be the new James Bond so I said yeah, okay I'll give it a whirl and the next thing you know they're flying me off to Miami for a screen test with the ten most beautiful women in the world. Hang about, I said—how can they be the ten most beautiful women in the world—my mother isn't here.

Mrs Hinson Why can't you ever give a straight answer to a straight question?

David More interesting if you make it up as you go along—I mean, look at Dad's shed.

Mrs Hinson You don't half talk rubbish at times.

David No, truth is I've been up to my eyes.

Mrs Hinson Oh yes? (*Her mouth tightens, prune-like*)

David Anyway, nice to see you making use of the garden.

Mrs Hinson It's one of the few pleasures I've got left since your poor dear father passed away.

The mobile telephone rings

Mrs Hinson (*immediately/imperiously*) Phone!

David (*on the phone*) Hello? . . . Oh, hello Keith, what's the problem? . . . Uh-huh . . . Uh-huh . . . (*He cups the phone; to Mrs Hinson*) One of my managers . . .

David absently goes into the shed as he listens and closes the door after him

Mrs Hinson gives a cynical little jerk of the head and takes up the "TV Times" to read as:

Michael enters and takes the collapsed rotary line behind the shed. There is some banging about and subdued cursing. Then he reappears, sucking his finger as:

Roma comes out of the kitchen

Michael Oh—yes—I forgot to tell you, when I was on my run this morning I suddenly heard this little voice in my head saying hang on, Smethurst, go via Carthew Road. And what do I see? A skip being delivered to number eight—the late Victorian one.

Roma Well done, Mickey!

Michael Keep your eye on it, okay?

Roma What is it we're looking for, specifically?

Michael Architraving for the upstairs hall.

Roma Right. (*She makes to go in*) Wasn't it from Carthew Road you recovered the tables?

Michael No—the chimney pots.

Roma I thought it was the tables.

Michael No, the tables were Morrison Avenue.

Roma Where you recovered the skirting?

Michael No, the skirting was Mafeking Close.

Roma Ah—yes—right. Anyway—well done, Mickey.

Roma goes into the kitchen

Michael (*to himself*) There's something else, I'm sure there is.

Michael goes into the kitchen as:

David comes out of the shed

David Sorry about that—business.

Mrs Hinson Oh yes?

David Why don't you sit in a proper chair?

Mrs Hinson Because of my back, that's why.

David pulls an old-fashioned deckchair out of the shed. He puts down the telephone and sets up the chair as:

Mrs Hinson Going on about my step, all I have ever tried to do—migraine or no migraine—is keep a home fit for human habitation.

David Yeah, well, I can't fault you there, Mum.

Michael enters with a screwdriver. Throughout the following he tightens the screws on one of the trestle hinges

Mrs Hinson Not that these things mean much to you anymore.

David No, no—we're heavily into squalor. (*He sits in the deckchair and lights a thin cigar using a slim gold lighter*) Anyway, we're really happy there. It's a really nice house. Got a good feel about it.

Mrs Hinson I don't know why you moved. I suppose it was Madam's idea.

David It was our idea and the name is Jennifer.

Mrs Hinson Well she's not exactly one for soap and water, whatever her name is.

David Gonna make me a cup of tea, are you?

Mrs Hinson Give me a chance, you've only just got here.
David I'll put the kettle on.
Mrs Hinson I'll do it, I'll do it.

Nevertheless she makes no effort to stop him

   David goes into the kitchen as:

   Roma comes out of the kitchen, now wearing a small pinny and kitchen gloves

Roma Michael . . . you didn't take the food out of the freezer.
Michael (*remembering*) Damn.
Roma *Mickey*.
Michael I was just going to do it when Nick phoned. I knew there was something. Damn and blast.

   Roma gives him an old-fashioned look and goes inside as:

   David comes out

   Michael continues to tighten up the hinges

Mrs Hinson I wish you'd telephone before you come.
David You never answer.
Mrs Hinson I answer the telephone when it's important.
David No point in having a phone if you don't answer it—how do I know something hasn't happened to you?
Mrs Hinson You've got enough on your plate without me running up a huge phone bill.
David (*patiently*) Mum, where's the sense in me having to phone Mrs Whittaker over the road and asking her to check you're all right when you've got a perfectly good phone of your own but you just won't use it?
Mrs Hinson (*firmly*) That telephone is for emergencies. I am not using it like a public convenience. 'Course, I know *you* can't move an inch without your precious talkie-walkie sticking out of your ear.
David (*grinning and stretching his arms above his head*) Gotta keep in touch, Mum, gotta keep in touch.

   Roma enters

Roma Mickey, I really do need your opinion.
Michael Coming, coming.

   Roma exits

   Michael follows her

Mrs Hinson And I'll tell you something else, you've lost weight.
David I hope so. (*He pats his stomach*)
Mrs Hinson I suppose she's got you on another one of them diets.
David No solids, no fluids.
Mrs Hinson When did you last have a decent meal?
David I'm fine.

Mrs Hinson (*struggling to her feet*) I'm going to make you a nice sandwich.
David No, honest Mum, just a biscuit.
Mrs Hinson Biscuits won't do you much good.
David Cuppa tea and a nice biscuit. (*He winks at her and settles in the chair, knowing she loves it*)
Mrs Hinson I'm not one of your skivvies, you know. (*She makes to hobble away, making dramatic use of the frame, but suddenly plants a brief kiss on top of his head*) You're a good boy, David. I don't know why they can't leave you in peace, really I don't. (*And behind his back she takes up the frame and moves briskly to the kitchen*)

Mrs Hinson exits

David remains in the deckchair, smoking. There is something on his mind and he glances at his watch as:

Michael and Roma enter

He is carrying a fourteen pound block of cheddar cheese sealed in plastic and clearly marked in black pentel "Cheese—Cheddar"

She is carrying two cardboard boxes, one clearly marked "Chops—Pork" and the other "Sausages—Pork"

Roma It will defrost in time, won't it?
Michael The thing is, of course, it should never have been put in the freezer like this in the first place. It should have been separated into individual portions and put in little bags, not just shoved in in one great big lump.

Roma opens her mouth to point out that she did suggest this, but thinks better of it

They put down the food and throughout the following, set about moving and erecting one of the trestle tables. We now see that it is old and has been extensively repaired with new hinges etc. The truth is, not much of the original remains

Roma This is where a microwave would have come into its own, of course.
Michael (*not heavily*) You're not still nagging me about a microwave.
Roma No, but times like this do rather tend to prove my point.
Michael I shall get you your microwave just as soon as I find time to compare specifications. These things aren't cheap and I'm sure you wouldn't want me to unbalance the books for the sake of a dozen or so frozen sausages— or perhaps you would, I'm never sure with you anymore.
Roma Don't be a bully. (*She tickles him—one of their 'fun things'*)

The telephone rings

Michael Off you go, I can manage.

Roma exits through the french windows as:

Michael continues erecting the table. It proves quite a challenge. He catches his finger and curses loudly

Hearing the curse David wanders over to the fence. Standing on tiptoe he glances over to see Michael abusing the table

Michael catches sight of David

David How d'you do?
Michael Good-afternoon.

David makes to move away from the fence

I say . . .

Both men stand and face each other over the fence

During the following Roma can be seen using a cordless telephone behind the french windows

I wonder if I might have a word with Mrs——
David Hinson.
Michael Hinson—yes of course—Mrs Hinson. Hinson, Hinson, Hinson. And you are?
David David Hinson Hinson Hinson. The pride and joy. The son.
Michael (*dawning*) Ah, yes—hello—Smethurst—Michael—we moved in about, oh, two months ago.
David Yeah, we noticed.
Michael Why I wanted to speak to—er—we're having a little gathering here this evening. No, as you were, quite a large gathering in fact. A housewarming.
David Very nice.
Michael My point being that it's bound to be something of a thrash and if the weather holds good which I'm assured it will, we'll mostly be out here in the garden.
David Got the picture; not a dry throat in the house—right, Michael?
Michael I have no intention of letting things get out of hand of course but there are always those who abuse hospitality as I'm sure you appreciate.
David Only too well, Michael, only too well.
Michael We have, um, we have *tried* to inform your mother but she seems unwilling to answer the door.
David I have the same trouble.
Michael Anyway, as long as you're——
David Very kind of you to give us the S.P., Michael.

Michael finds this constant and easy use of his name quite unnerving

Michael Oh yes—one other thing—when I was up on the roof the other day—renewing my guttering—I noticed there's a bit of a crack opening up in your wall. (*He points*)

David looks up briefly

Not settlement, I hope?
David No, no, we had an earthquake—just before you moved in—I'm surprised your surveyor didn't mention it.

It takes a moment for Michael to realise it is a joke

Michael Ah. Yes. Ha!

David That your game then, is it, Michael?

Michael Game?

David The building trade. I mean—(*indicating*) from what you've done to the house . . .

Michael (*catching on*) Good god no, I'm a doctor.

David (*"impressed"*) A doctor.

Michael At Saint Bernard's.

David (*grinning*) I wouldn't mention that to my mother if I were you, Michael, you'll never see the back of her.

Michael (*not really understanding why*) Oh—yes—right.

David So, the old do-it-yourself's by way of relaxation—is that it?

Michael I did pretty much all the work on the house, actually.

David Get away.

Michael You do it yourself, you know it's done properly, right?

David You mean you did the plumbing and bricklaying and——

Michael Everything.

David (*pointing*) The patio as well?

Michael Everything.

David Well I take my hat off to you, Michael. (*He beckons him closer*) Here, you—er—you didn't come across the body by any chance?

Michael The what?

David Pulling your leg, Michael, pulling your leg, although there is supposed to be some buried treasure. Obviously the Barretts didn't mention it.

Mrs Hinson (*calling; off*) David!

David Anyway. Nice talking to you, Michael—enjoy your party. (*He moves towards the kitchen*)

Mrs Hinson appears with a tea tray

Michael watches for a moment, then sets about tightening the screws on another trestle

Michael then goes round to the shed and moves out of sight as:

David takes the tray to the garden table, followed by Mrs Hinson who makes painful use of the walking frame which no longer holds the basket. They both sit

Bloke next door says to tell you they're having a party tonight

Mrs Hinson When?

David Just now. He stuck his head over.

Mrs Hinson Oh yes? (*A sudden thought*) I hope you behaved yourself, my son.

David We had a very interesting little chat as it happens.

Mrs Hinson You had a very interesting little chat with Mrs Barrett when *they* moved in, I seem to remember.

David (*a slow grin as he remembers*) Oh yeah . . .

Mrs Hinson Nine years old you were and you're just as daft now. (*With a jerk of the head*) Telling her there was an unexploded bomb in the garden. You didn't tell him that, did you?

David Now would I?

Mrs Hinson Yes—well—I certainly wouldn't put it past you. (*A sudden thought*) What's he mean—a party?

David A party. A jolly-up.

Mrs Hinson (*with a jerk of the head*) More banging around. That's all I've had for weeks—bang, bang, bang.

David They've certainly knocked the old place about a bit.

Mrs Hinson Makes me laugh. All the old-fashioned stuff your father took out, they're paying a fortune to have put back in again. Round and round, everything goes round and round.

David It's called gentrification.

Mrs Hinson Yes, well, whatever it's called it makes too much noise. Sometimes I've sat in there trying to watch the television with my head reeling.

David You should have said something.

Mrs Hinson I shouldn't have to.

David I'll have a word before I go.

Mrs Hinson Too late now. Anyway, I've never spoken to him. Spoke to *her*. She caught me the other day—I was sweeping my path. (*She does her 'posh' accent*) "Oh hello" she says, "I'm so glad I've caught you at last. I have been knocking but you don't seem to answer." "That's because I don't know who it is," I said. "Well anyway," she says, "My name is Mrs whatever-it-was——

David Bracegirdle.

Mrs Hinson —and I just want to introduce myself and apologise for the noise and if there's ever anything I can do." "Like what," I said. "Like doing some shopping for you," she says, "Or posting your letters." "That's quite all right, Mrs whatever-your-name is——"

David Bracegirdle.

Mrs Hinson —I said—I like to get my own bits and pieces when I collect my pension and I haven't written a letter since my sister Lily moved to Ramsgate, God rest her soul. "Oh," she says. "Well," she says. And that's the last I've seen of her.

David Well, well, I wonder why? (*He picks up a biscuit*)

Mrs Hinson thrusts the plate at him

Mrs Hinson Take the plate—come on, you look half-starved.

He does not bother to argue as:

Michael comes out from behind the shed and erects the trestle table

Roma comes out with three trays which they will put the food on and then they take the lids off the two boxes. They always enjoy working together as a team

Roma Guess who that was?

Michael Was what?

Roma On the phone. Cheese.

Michael No idea.

Roma Gareth. Chops.

Michael Don't tell me, he and Sandy have had another row.

Roma It must be so tiring. All that arguing, all that—emotion. Sausages.

Michael Beats me how they ever got together.

Roma Sex, I'm afraid.

Michael Yes, I suppose so. If only people would think *past* it.

Roma Probably just as well they're not coming, actually. I mean, any sort of gathering and Gareth *always* gets drunk and he and Sandy *always* have a fight—mind you, it does rather mess up our numbers. I mean, that's Nick and Gilly and Gareth and Sandy——

Michael Oh no, there are bound to be gatecrashers once word gets round. Probably have trouble keeping the buggers out.

Roma (*lowering her voice*) Who was that next door by the way?

Michael The son.

Roma Oh, that was the *son*.

Michael Derek I think he said.

Roma David.

Michael Sure he said Derek.

Roma No, David. The Neighbourhood Watch chappie mentioned him— apparently he's doing rather well for himself—quite how I've yet to discover.

Michael Yes, he obviously has money. Struck me as the scrap metal type.

Roma And you did tell him about the party.

Michael Oh yes, no trouble there. Now then, what's next on the agenda?

Roma You to collect the wine, me to make a start on the potato salad.

Michael The wine—right. (*He makes for the kitchen*) I hope they remember to bring a bottle, these people.

Roma Of course they will, it's on the invitation and anyway, people *do*.

Michael exits into the kitchen

(*Calling after him*) I was wondering though, Mickey, if it might not be a good idea—as it's a new one—to assemble the barbecue first—just in case—you know.

Michael appears in the kitchen doorway, a hand behind his back

Michael (*mock-heavy*) Roma, you promised. And what do I find? (*He produces a half-eaten biscuit from behind his back*) You've been nibbling.

Roma Just one little biscuit.

Michael You promised me and you've been nibbling.

Roma One little biscuit made with vegetable oil.

Michael (*advancing on her*) Yes, but you promised me and what do I find, eh —eh? What else do you get up to behind my back, eh—eh? (*He puts the biscuit between his teeth and tickles her*)

She giggles as he tickles with one hand and makes a big play of eating the biscuit with the other

Roma Not fair! Not fair!

She tickles him and gets the biscuit from him

Roma runs into the kitchen

Michael chases Roma through the kitchen into the sitting-room and out through the french windows into the garden, then back into the kitchen, and round and out through the french windows again, with Michael crying, "Put that down!"

While Roma shrieks "Give, give!" as she is finally caught and tickled

The noises travel loud and clear to next door. Mrs Hinson gets up, still holding her cup, and moves to bend at the fence, trying to look through a peephole in it

David (*grinning*) You still use the old peephole, then.
Mrs Hinson (*waving to him*) Ssshhh . . .

At the same time, Michael and Roma have become aware of the noise they have been making. Each now has a bit of biscuit in their mouth. They put fingers exaggeratedly to their lips and "creep" to the fence to listen for any reaction from next door

For a moment the three of them are bent at the fence, listening

Mrs Hinson holding her cup

Roma and Michael holding their biscuits

Then Roma and Michael exit and tiptoe inside

Mrs Hinson (*returning to her chair*) If you ask me, it's worse than living on the continent.
David Tell you what, you make a lovely cuppa tea. (*He kisses his fingers and blows her a kiss*) Lo mejor, mamita.
Mrs Hinson You're just like your father, an old sprucer
David (*grinning*) Yeah. (*Smiling at the memory*) Good old Dad.
Mrs Hinson I always knew when he was after something.
David But did he ever get it?
Mrs Hinson (*pretending to be deaf*) Par-don?

David gets up and moves to take a peek over the L fence

They're having a week's holiday.
David Still got the old motorbike I see.
Mrs Hinson Never goes anywhere on it. Just takes it apart in the garden and puts it back together again. Drives her mad.

David grins and sits

There is a pause

(*She can tell there is something on his mind*) So what are *you* after?
David Just thought I'd pop over and see how you are.
Mrs Hinson I'm exactly the same as I was when you popped over four weeks ago. Half an hour I think you stayed *and* glued to your talkie-walkie for most of that.

David I know and I really have been rushed off my feet, what with Jen being in hospital and opening the new shop—I did tell you we've opened a new shop, didn't I? Hampton Wick. Very high class with a delicatessen counter.
Mrs Hinson (*flatly*) Very nice.
David That's what I like about you, Mum—always in the corner, cheering.
Mrs Hinson Eat your biscuits and don't be so argumentative, I'm your mother.

David wanders over to the old shed and looks through the window. He smiles to himself at his memories

David The old shed needs a bit of a clear-out.
Mrs Hinson Don't you dare touch your father's shed.
David Have to give it a go sooner or later.
Mrs Hinson Why?
David (*considering*) Dunno really. Yeah, you're right. (*He moves back*) Any more tea in that pot?
Mrs Hinson (*struggling to her feet and collecting the frame*) It'll be stone-cold, I'll make some fresh, bring the tray, will you? (*She starts to move to the kitchen*) What did you say their name was?
David Bracegirdle. Wayne and Sharon Bracegirdle.
Mrs Hinson Bracegirdle?
David Sharon and Wayne.

Mrs Hinson gives a derisive jerk of her head

Mrs Hinson (*using the same tone as if they'd got leprosy*) They've got twins.
David Yeah—he struck me as the sort of bloke who doesn't do things by half.

David and Mrs Hinson exit into the kitchen as:

Michael and Roma come out of the kitchen under the weight of a large package which they bring out into the garden. They move around with the box during the following as Michael decides where he wants to put it, Roma's arms getting heavier and heavier

Roma What we will have to come to a decision about, Mike, is ashtrays.
Michael Careful of the shrub.
Roma Oh, yes. (*To the shrub*) Sorry Mister Shrub. (*To Michael*) If we put them out we'll only be encouraging people and if we don't those that do will only stub them out wherever they fancy—what d'you think?
Michael Well I certainly intend discouraging smoking in the house.
Roma Absolutely.
Michael People *do* know how we feel.
Roma I wonder then if it might not be an idea to designate the garden as the smoking area and put an ashtray or two but certainly no more—out here.
Michael Out here and well away from the food.
Roma Good idea, Mike—*smashing*.
Michael In fact, I think we should encourage people to stay in the garden as much as possible. They can do less damage out here which reminds me—

we shall need to keep a very close eye on the greenery—(*to the shrub*) isn't that so, old chap?
Roma They will want to look around the house though, Mike. I mean I take your point but it is a housewarming.
Michael Yes, but I'm not having them sneaking off on their own. Look around the house by all means *but* in a controlled situation. (*Positioning the box*) Here I think. No as you were—here.

They set down the box

Roma exits into the kitchen

He tears open the cardboard package—it isn't easy—and takes out the various components that will make up a barbecue with a hood and a wheeled tripod stand

Michael will go into the kitchen and reappear with his toolbox and set about erecting the barbecue, whilst reading from the instruction sheet as:

David comes out of the kitchen with a cup of tea

Mrs Hinson follows him and goes to the line to see how her washing is drying. She takes down a pair of stockings and rolls them up as:

Mrs Hinson Where've you been, anyway? Playing golf I suppose.
David Not today.
Mrs Hinson I thought Saturdays she let you play golf.
David She's my wife and she's called Jennifer.

Roma comes out of the kitchen and tests the food to see if the sun is taking effect as:

Mrs Hinson Your Rosemary used to like you playing golf.
David I'm not married to Rosemary any more.
Mrs Hinson No, you're not and more's the pity.
David Yes, well, we know all about that, don't we?
Mrs Hinson She used to love you playing golf, your Rosemary.

The Smethurst telephone rings

(*Instantly and imperiously*) Phone!

Michael and Roma react to the sound of her voice

Roma goes in through the french windows as:

Mrs Hinson Well in my opinion you should have had a game of golf. All this running about, making decisions, your brain won't stand it. Where is Madam, anyway?
David Jennifer.
Mrs Hinson Having her hair done again I suppose.
David As a matter of fact she's down the road—getting you some shopping.
Mrs Hinson Down the road?
David She dropped me off and took the car straight on. (*Looking at his watch*) Should be here any minute.

Mrs Hinson's mouth tightens at the news

Mrs Hinson I see.

Roma appears at the french windows, cupping the telephone receiver

Roma It's Angela. One of Jerry's Japanese clients has got tickets for *Les Miserables* tonight and they daren't say no.
Michael Soddit!

He has hurt his finger but she misconstrues his reply

Roma They're terribly sorry.
Michael (*sucking his finger*) Tell her it's a pity he's not here now.
Roma (*into the phone; brightly*) Mickey says to tell you it's a pity Jerry isn't here now.
Michael Not Jerry—his client.
Roma (*into the phone*) Correction—not Jerry, his client. (*She laughs gaily, but cups the receiver*) Why?
Michael Because being Japanese he could have helped me make sense of these rotten instructions.

Roma gives him her old-fashioned look

Roma (*into the phone*) We've bought this new barbecue set you see and Mickey is having terrible trouble with the . . .

Roma exits

David D'you know—never once have you asked me how she is.
Mrs Hinson How who is?
David Jennifer. You know she's been in hospital but——
Mrs Hinson I don't have to ask—you tell me.
David Wouldn't it have been nice if you'd asked?
Mrs Hinson Well it can't have been anything serious or they wouldn't have let her out so quick. I mean, I might not know much, my son, but one thing you cannot fault me on is my intimate knowledge of the National Health Service.
David That's what I was trying to tell the bloke next door.
Mrs Hinson Par-don?
David Nothing.
Mrs Hinson Besides, all I get from you is she's being inspected.
David Examined.
Mrs Hinson Well, whatever it is. No wonder she can't get pregnant, all this poking about she authorises.
David (*for the umpteenth time*) We do not—want—children—okay?

The Hinson doorbell rings

Mrs Hinson Door!

Michael reacts to her shout

David That'll be Jen. (*He moves to the kitchen door*) And Mum—be nice, eh? For *my* sake.

David goes indoors

Mrs Hinson (*calling after him*) I was going to make you a nice rice pudding! (*She glowers*) Trust her to spoil it.

Michael moves to take a peek over the fence

Mrs Hinson (*catching him*) Can I help you?

Michael Oh—yes—good-afternoon, Mrs—umm. (*He stands on tiptoe*) Sorry to disturb you—what I should have said—just in case you—umm —it's fancy dress. Tonight. The party.

Mrs Hinson (*down her nose*) Oh yes?

Michael Yes. Actually, we're having a theme. For the fancy dress. Famous couples in reverse.

Mrs Hinson Oh yes?

Michael By that I mean the chap takes the part of the female of the pair and the wife or girlfriend or whatever takes the part of the male.

Mrs Hinson Oh yes?

Michael So if you think of a famous couple like, say——

Mrs Hinson Roy Rogers and Trigger.

Michael Roy Rogers and Trigger . . . The girl will take the part of Roy Rogers and the chap will take the part of—Trigger. (*He frowns. There's something not quite right here*) Anyway. Just wanted to keep you informed —sorry to disturb you.

Mrs Hinson I say—. (*She moves nearer the fence*) I had a milkman once called Bracegirdle. No relation by any chance, was he?

Michael Ummm . . .

Mrs Hinson His mother kept rabbits under their kitchen table.

Michael Really?

Mrs Hinson That's how it stuck in my mind.

Michael Sorry—what did?

Mrs Hinson *Bracegirdle.*

Michael Oh—yes—right. I'll let you get on then. Well done. (*He goes back to erecting the barbecue*)

Mrs Hinson looks towards the house and moves nippily to take up her walking frame so that she is slowly moving towards her washing as:

Jennifer appears in the french windows. She's in her late 30s, attractive middle-class and wears good casual clothing. She carries a large bunch of cut flowers. She watches Mrs Hinson, preparing herself for what she clearly sees as an ordeal

Michael (*to himself; suddenly*) Bracegirdle, what's she on about, Bracegirdle? (*He goes to the fence and gets on tiptoe to speak to Mrs Hinson, but he sees Jennifer and goes back to his work, still trying to work out what she was on about*)

Jennifer Hello Mum. How *are* you? Nice to see you.

Mrs Hinson Nice to see *you*, dear.

They kiss without quite touching. They are so "nice" to each other it hurts

Jennifer (*holding out the flowers*) I brought you some flowers.
Mrs Hinson Oh you shouldn't have, they'll only die.
Jennifer Oh, they'll be all right if you don't breathe on them—I'll put them in a vase for you, shall I?
Mrs Hinson Yes please, dear, thank you. And you've been getting some shopping for me, I understand.
Jennifer David's bringing it in now.
Mrs Hinson He's a good boy, my David. (*She beckons Jennifer closer and speaks in a manner more mouthing than actually saying the words. This is her way of talking "delicate"*) I think he looks very tired.
Jennifer Do you?
Mrs Hinson You know—mentally. I think he could do with a good holiday myself. It must be a terrible strain, being executive. Still, you're a great help to him. I know you are. When you're fit. (*She suddenly remembers and indicates the deckchair*) Sit down, dear, you look exhausted.

David appears in the kitchen doorway, holding a box of provisions

David I'll put this stuff away, all right? (*He starts to go inside–clearly wanting to stay out of the way*)
Jennifer Put these in acid for your mother, will you, darling? (*She puts the flowers on top of the box and smiles flatly at him*)

David inwardly groans and takes the box into the kitchen

Mrs Hinson (*calling*) And put the kettle on, will you Son?
Jennifer (*calling*) Not for me, thanks.
Mrs Hinson Oh no, you prefer something stronger, don't you dear? Ask David to have a look in the sideboard, there might be a droppa port or something left over from Christmas.
Jennifer (*smiling sweetly*) I'll try to manage without, but it was a lovely thought, thanks Mum.

They "smile" at each other

Mrs Hinson (*sitting "painfully"*) I would have visited you in hospital but David intimated that he'd rather see you all to himself.
Jennifer Yes, he can be very forceful. (*She sits in the deckchair*)
Mrs Hinson (*"delicate" again*) He never told me what it was, you know. Didn't want to worry me, I expect. Something internal, was it dear?
Jennifer Vaguely.
Mrs Hinson Yes, it's usually internal with a woman. (*Very confidentially*) Mine was internal, you know.
Jennifer (*"impressed"*) No I didn't.
Mrs Hinson That was before all these drugs of course. (*She sucks in the air dramatically, re-living the moment*) I could have gone either way. Apparently the entire profession was dumbfounded. Now then—(*she struggles to her feet and collects the frame*) you make yourself comfortable

while I see how my David's getting on in the kitchen. You know what they're like—helpless and hopeless. (*She starts to move towards the kitchen*) He shouldn't have to *be* in the kitchen, a man in his position.

Mrs Hinson exits

Once Mrs Hinson is out of her view Jennifer's smile fades. She reaches into her handbag and takes out a packet of cigarettes. She is sorely tempted but she is trying to give up. She makes the effort and shoves the packet back again as:

Roma comes out of the kitchen and goes directly to the food

Michael finishes erecting the barbecue

Michael There.
Roma Oh that's smashing, Mike, well done.
Michael Now then, where to put it.
Roma We should certainly keep it away from—(*she indicates and, quietly:*) next door. Over here somewhere, d'you think? (*She indicates the other side of the garden*)
Michael (*wheeling the barbecue around*) Here—no, as you were, round the side out of everyone's way. (*He indicates the side of the shed*)
Roma Oh that's much better, Mike, a really good idea—well done.

Michael wheels the barbecue round the shed and out of sight as:

Roma moves to look at the food

Mike, I really am terribly worried about the meat.

Michael reappears

Michael The what?
Roma The chops. And the sausages. They're still stuck together as hard as rock—they won't defrost in time, I know they won't.

Michael comes to have a look in the boxes

Michael (*prodding the meat in the box with his finger*) Mmm.
Roma And the cheese. It's completely solid.
Michael (*prodding the cheese in the box*) Mmm.

They stand looking down at the boxes for a moment

Okay, so here's the way I see it. We give it another quarter of an hour and then—(*he takes up one of the boxes and drops it from a height of about three inches back onto the table. He looks hopefully into the box*) we gently drop it and—with any luck—the vibration will—shake it apart. Okay? (*He briefly kisses her brow*) Don't worry about it. (*Looking at his watch*) Now then—wine.

Michael exits

Roma remains looking down at the food, unconvinced

Roma (*calling after him*) What about the cheese? I mean, you can't vibrate *cheese* to pieces, surely?

Roma exits hurrying as:

David ambles out of the kitchen

Jennifer Is the car all right where it is?

David Someone'll knock if it isn't.

Jennifer There was a man across the road giving me some terrible looks.

David (*grins*) That'll be old Paddy McMonagle. He's all right. When he's sober.

There is a pause

Jennifer Have you said anything to her?

David Not yet.

Jennifer (*more resigned than annoyed*) I knew it.

David Haven't had the chance.

Jennifer The whole idea was for me to stay out of the way so that you could say something.

David And I was going to—(*he kisses her brow*)—she had one of her turns.

Jennifer She doesn't have turns.

David I nearly had to give her the kiss of life——

Jennifer Why do you do it?

David —fighting for breath she was.

Jennifer Can't face something, turn it into a joke.

David It's difficult.

Jennifer All right, I'll do it, the Wicked Witch.

David I'll do it.

There is a pause

I was born in this house.

Jennifer That's no reason why she should die in it.

David looks at her

Is it?

There is a pause. Then he smiles and she extends her arms. He moves to bend over the chair and she enfolds him in her arms. They kiss as:

Mrs Hinson enters

Mrs Hinson (*jokily enough but she means it*) All right you two lovebirds, that's enough of that.

Jennifer (*brightly*) Ah there you are, Mum—come and sit down. (*She keeps hold of David's hand—a defiant show of affection*)

Mrs Hinson moves to sit in her chair, making painful use of the frame

We were just saying how nice the garden looks.

Mrs Hinson indicates that she needs help to sit so that David has to let go of Jennifer's hand and finds himself holding his mother's hand as:

Mrs Hinson It's not a patch on what it was when my hubbie was alive. He loved this garden, my hubbie. Kept it spotless.

David Who cut the grass?

Mrs Hinson I had to pay that young wassisname fifty pence.

Jennifer That's the problem, you see, Mum, he'd like to keep the garden nice for you—wouldn't you, David—but living so far away . . .

Mrs Hinson (*to David; patting his hand*) That's all right, Son, I quite understand.

Jennifer Of course, if you lived *nearer* . . .

Jennifer looks pointedly at David who avoids her eyes and looks up at the house

Mrs Hinson What are you looking at?

David Bloke next door says there's a crack in the wall—oh yeah, I see it—I'd better get someone round.

Mrs Hinson Why d'you need to get someone round?

David In case it gets worse.

Mrs Hinson Your poor dear father wouldn't have got someone round.

David No, he wouldn't.

Mrs Hinson He would have filled that crack in himself—even if it meant staying up all night.

Jennifer *Especially* if it meant staying up all night.

Mrs Hinson Par-don?

David (*cupping an ear*) Sorry?

Mrs Hinson Well if you are going to get someone round, you can get him to have a look at the lock on my bathroom door.

David Why, what's wrong with it?

Mrs Hinson It gets stuck.

David Right. (*He has an amusing thought*) I'll get the bloke next door to do it.

Jennifer How are you getting on with the new neighbours?

Mrs Hinson You know me, Jennifer, speak when I'm spoken to and not before.

Jennifer You've never been one to interfere.

Mrs Hinson Although I did hear that the husband might be related to my old milkman.

Jennifer Really?

Mrs Hinson Mr Bracegirdle.

Roma comes out of the kitchen. She goes directly to the food, and peers into the boxes. She takes one and drops it onto the table. She does it again and looks into the box. It isn't working. Somewhat guiltily, she takes one of the boxes and drops it from knee-height onto the paving, still without the desired effect. She goes back inside the house as:

Jennifer There seem to be so many new people in the street.

David Yeah, all changing. Whole area.

Mrs Hinson There's a ballet dancer moved in at number twenty-eight.

Jennifer Nice?

Mrs Hinson I've never spoken to him. But I did hear his friend drives a lorry for Tate and Lyle.

David I see old Mrs Parker's place is on the market.

Mrs Hinson Rumour has it that son of hers is shoving her off into one of these homes. That's all the thanks you get.

Jennifer looks at David

Jennifer Well—these houses aren't big—but living on your own, once you get to a certain age . . .

Mrs Hinson (*animal instinct. Changing the subject*) I tell you what, Jennifer, you've lost weight.

Jennifer Nearly six pounds.

Mrs Hinson (*sucking in air*) You'll need building up then—can't have the pair of you walking about looking half-starved. I tell you what I'm going to do . . .

Mrs Hinson struggles to her feet assisted by Jennifer and David

I'm going to make you a nice pudding to take home, that'll build you up a bit. Oh no, you don't like my puddings, do you, dear?

Jennifer Sorry.

Mrs Hinson Not your fault, dear, I expect my David will manage to force it down, he really misses my puddings, don't you, son? Here—(*to Jennifer, confidentially*) that last wife of his, that Rosemary, she was a strange one she was, couldn't cook for toffee. Mind you, she did his shirts beautiful.

Mrs Hinson begins an exaggeratedly-painful journey to the kitchen and parks the frame outside the kitchen door

Mrs Hinson exits into the kitchen

Jennifer When are you going to say something?

David No rush, is there?

Jennifer takes up her hand bag and pulls out her cigarettes

Jennifer And you can tell her from me she won't get any sympathy dragging that pile of scaffolding around.

David She's got a bad hip.

Jennifer That was a year ago. I spoke to the doctor, remember, she doesn't need it, he'd prefer her not to use it. It might work with you, it doesn't work with *me*. (*Pause*) Five minutes with her, and listen to me.

David gently takes away the cigarettes and kisses her brow

David Calm—down.

Jennifer I try, I really do try. (*She even manages a little smile*)

David She's not that bad.

Jennifer She's awful.

David She's an old lady and she's my mother.

Mrs Hinson appears in the kitchen doorway

Mrs Hinson David—come and help me get this lid off, there's a good boy.

Mrs Hinson goes back inside

David looks at Jennifer and shrugs

Jennifer Off you go—(*she flutters her fingers at him*) there's a good boy.
David (*with an open-handed gesture*) You see? You just won't let it go.

Jennifer watches David go, annoyed with herself

David exits

Jennifer wanders around the garden and becomes interested in the pond, disturbing the water with her toe as:

Roma comes out with the kitchen steps and a biscuit which she is furtively and quickly eating. She sets up the steps, takes up one of the boxes, and climbs to the top of the steps, holding the box as high as she can above her head

Jennifer turns to watch Roma, who is elevated over the fenceline

Roma is about to drop the box when she realises that she is being watched by Jennifer who is trying to work out what she is up to

Roma (*remaining at the top of the steps with the box over her head*) Good afternoon.
Jennifer Isn't it—yes—beautiful.
Roma (*lowers the box*) We've had a slight mishap with the deep freeze.
Jennifer Oh I see . . .
Roma Well—bad planning really—not like us at all.

There is a slight pause

Jennifer How are you settling in?
Roma Oh, we love it.
Jennifer Yes, they're nice little houses.
Roma (*lightly*) Not so little actually. Do you—umm . . . ?
Jennifer No, no, we're out at Shepperton.
Roma On the river?
Jennifer Near the river.
Roma Smashing.

There is a slight pause

Roma Mrs Hinson wouldn't by any chance have a microwave, would she?
Jennifer 'Fraid not. Sorry.
Roma We will be getting one of course but Mickey does so enjoy his comparative studies.
Jennifer Aha.
Roma Of course, we could just go out and buy one but—you know— impulse buying—fatal.
Jennifer Nice though.

They smile at each other

Michael (*off; yelling*) Roma!
Roma Coming! Do excuse me.

Roma hurries down the steps, puts the box on the table and carries the steps into the kitchen as:

David comes out of the Hinson kitchen and sits in the deckchair as:

Jennifer Do you want me to cancel tonight or what?
David Why, what's happening?
Jennifer We're having Kay and John over for dinner.
David What time?
Jennifer Seven o'clock.
David Give'em a ring—make it eight. He won't mind, he's trying to get some business out of me.
Jennifer (*glancing over the fence; speaking quietly*) Did your mother say he was a milkman?
David Who?

Jennifer indicates next door as Roma comes out of the kitchen and moves stealthily to peer through the hole in the fence

Err—(*but he can't resist*) yeah—why?
Jennifer I've just spoken to his wife—I assume it was his wife.
David And?
Jennifer She was standing on top of a ladder holding a box over her head.

She demonstrates

Mrs Hinson comes out of the kitchen as:

The Smethurst telephone rings

Mrs Hinson Phone!

Roma jerks upright and hurries indoors

Jennifer That reminds me—(*she takes up the mobile telephone from the table*) I must phone Kay.

Jennifer goes inside, mouthing to David to "talk to her". During the following she looks through the french windows as she uses the phone

Mrs Hinson (*suspiciously*) What's she up to?
David She's not up to anything.
Mrs Hinson If you ask me, she's up to something.
David (*sitting next to her*) Mum—we're worried about you. Both of us.
Mrs Hinson What d'you mean, worried about me?
David Being here. On your own.
Mrs Hinson (*her mouth tightens*) I see.
David You're not getting any younger—what happens if you have another fall?
Mrs Hinson I'm quite capable, thank you.
David Yes, but are you? (*A moment*) Mum—I want you to sell the house and move into a little flat—with no stairs to worry about—near us.

Mrs Hinson What you mean is, you want me in one of them homes. That's why you've come here, isn't it, to get me into one of them homes.

David Mum it's nothing like that—we've already found you a little——

Mrs Hinson That's right, gang up on me. I knew we should never have sent you to that grammar school. If your poor father could hear the way you're talking to me now. (*She pulls out her handkerchief, doing her close to tears performance*)

David already knows he's onto a loser

She blows into her handkerchief as:

Roma comes out into the garden, using the cordless telephone

The following speech is punctuated by Mrs Hinson's tearful assertions of "I knew it—I knew she was up to something"

Roma No of course we . . . Yes I will, he's just popped out to collect the wine . . . Say hello to Alan—and if you *can* get a babysitter, we'd be more than . . . Yes . . . Yes—'bye.

Roma switches off the telephone and stands for a moment, sucking in air and breathing deeply, with her shoulders heaving. She puts the phone in her tracksuit pocket

Roma exits through the french windows

David I'm sorry, Mum, I didn't mean to . . .

Mrs Hinson Springing it on me like that, you ought to have more sense——

David Yes I know, I——

Mrs Hinson —I don't like being rushed. I'm too old to be rushed. I'm your mother and this is my home.

David Just—have a think about it. That's all I ask. Just—have a think about it.

He takes her hand which will remain limp in his as:

Mrs Hinson I've never wanted to be the cause of any trouble.

David You're not.

Mrs Hinson I've only ever wanted to be helpful.

David Yes, I know you have. But let's face it, the whole street's changing. Most of your friends are either going or gone.

Mrs Hinson (*bravely*) Yes, all right son, I'll think about it. It's just a peculiar feeling, that's all. Being jettisoned by your own flesh and blood.

David It isn't like that.

Mrs Hinson Oh I think it is, Son, although I like to believe you was acting under orders.

Roma hurries out of the kitchen, prods the meat and goes straight to the shed where, unseen but heard she starts pulling things around as:

David Tell you what, come back with us.

Mrs Hinson What—now?

David Come back, have a look at the flat, and we can talk about it.

Mrs Hinson No.
David Why not?
Mrs Hinson Because I do not go where I am not wanted.
David You are wanted.
Mrs Hinson *You* know what I mean.
David Come on—come back with us. I want you to. (*He indicates next door*)
    Besides, if they're having music banging away all night.

Roma continues to bang around in the shed

Mrs Hinson You mean—stay?

David gets up

David (*shiftily*) Well—stay tonight anyway.
Mrs Hinson I see.
David Tonight—tomorrow night—see how things work out. Okay?

Mrs Hinson considers for a moment, but knows she's already got him where she wants him

Mrs Hinson Yes—all right, son—you know best.

He moves decisively to help her

David Right then.
Mrs Hinson I shall need to tidy up a bit first.
David Why?
Mrs Hinson Because.
David Mum, the only one liable to see the place is a burglar, why make it
    comfortable for him?
Mrs Hinson Don't talk so daft—besides, I'm making you a pudding.
David Listen—about that pudding.
Mrs Hinson (*glaring*) I've started and so I shall finish. (*She takes up her
    frame*)
David Don't—er—don't say anything to Jen. I'll let her know what's
    happening, okay?
Mrs Hinson I quite understand, son. (*She even manages to give him a dry peck
    on the cheek*) You're a good boy, I know you only try to do what's for the
    best, for all your funny ways. And it must be a terrible strain, being
    executive and having to cope with You-Know-Who. (*She begins her frame-
    assisted journey to the kitchen*) I shall have to take my *TV Times* though,
    they don't tell you half what you want to know in the paper.

Mrs Hinson goes inside, parking the frame

*David sees Jennifer looking at him through the french windows. He gives her a
big thumbs-up sign and then moves away and wanders into the shed as:*

*Roma appears from behind the shed with what she has been searching for—a
large club hammer. She carries it across to the food. She takes one of the
boxes and carefully sets it on the paving. She gets on her knees, raises the
hammer high, and is about to give the box an almighty wallop when:*

Michael appears in the doorway with a carton of wine

Michael They'd run out of the Bulgarian of course—yes I know, typical—so for the red I thought, well, can't do much better than the *Tonino Vino da Tavola*—it's still at two-thirty-four by the way—and for the white I thought we'd try the *Touraine Sauvignon*. It's more than I wanted to pay, two-ninety-nine, but he assures me it's—hang on, what's this?
Roma Nothing's defrosting.
Michael Not a hammer, Ro.
Roma It's solid.
Michael Yes, but not a *hammer*.
Roma Mickey . . .

The telephone rings

She passes the hammer to him and pulls the phone from her tracksuit pocket

Roma hurries inside, through the french windows

Michael puts down the hammer and carries the box into the kitchen. He returns and puts the hammer in the shed. While he is in there things can be heard falling on him. He will re-arrange them as:

Jennifer comes out of the french windows, with the mobile telephone

David comes out of the shed with a war time gas-mask

Jennifer Eight o'clock is fine. He's bringing some drawings over for you to look at.
David (*holding the gas mask up*) Uh-huh—look at this.
Jennifer What is it?
David A gas-mask. Never threw anything away, my old man. "If they tried it once, they can try it again, my son" (*He returns the gas-mask to the shed and holds up a fretwork pipe rack*) This was his fretwork period, circa fifty-three. He spent hours in this old shed.
Jennifer (*patiently*) What about your mother?
David Umm—yeah—everything's okay. (*He gives her a big reassuring smile and returns the piperack to the shed as:*)
Jennifer She's right about the bathroom lock, by the way—it's very stiff. I should hate to think of her getting stuck in there. On second thoughts though . . .

Mrs Hinson appears in the kitchen doorway

Mrs Hinson I say, David—help me down with my case, will you, there's a good boy.
Jennifer (*to David*) Case?
Mrs Hinson It's under the bed in your old room—I want to give it a good airing.
Jennifer *Case?*
David All right, Mum—give me a minute, will you?
Mrs Hinson Oh dear, I haven't spoken out of turn, have I? (*She clamps a hand to her mouth*)

Mrs Hinson "discreetly" goes back inside

David I invited her over so she could have a look at the flat—okay?
Jennifer (*flat*) What do you mean—invited her over?
David Just for tonight—that's reasonable enough, surely?
Jennifer We're seeing Kay and John tonight.
David So she'll have to watch television.
Jennifer When doesn't she watch television?
David I'm doing my best, all right? I'm doing my best.

There is a pause

Jennifer All right, but just for tonight. I mean it, David—just for tonight.
David Hey.

David kisses her gently and then goes inside

Jennifer stands for a moment and then sits in the deckchair. She takes up the "TV Times", and flicks through it without really seeing it, then realising what it is, she drops it as if it is diseased

Roma comes out of the french window as:

Michael comes out from behind the shed

Michael Who was that?
Roma Umm—my mother.
Michael What's happened?
Roma What? Oh—nothing—nothing, just to say the—er—the boys are fine.
Michael Of course they are. They'll be having fun—and we'll be having fun.
Roma (*somewhat uncertainly*) Yes.
Michael I know what you're thinking. You're thinking how quiet the house is without them. Well—another couple of hours and the joint will be really jumping. Right on man! (*He jives across the patio but stops and frowns*) Just as long as they don't jump on the vegetation. Which reminds me . . . (*He takes a peek over the fence and sees Jennifer*)

He moves back out of sight, but Jennifer instinctively senses she has been looked at and looks in his direction

(*Quietly*) Is that their car outside?
Roma I don't know, is it?
Michael Someone's taken my parking space and I've had to park over the road where that lunatic Irishman likes to put his dreaded Dormobile—so no doubt sooner or later I'll be getting the usual mouthful of abuse.
Roma Mickey, I wonder if we shouldn't invite them over this evening.
Michael *Him*?
Roma Not Mr McMonagle—no. I mean next door. Just for a quick drink or something. Just to be—you know—a spot of PR.
Michael You mean Mrs—the old woman? Oh no. No no.
Roma There's the son. And his wife. She seems rather nice, actually.

Michael indicates that "she" is in the garden

Roma takes a peek through the spy-hole in the fence and Michael peeks over

Michael Lady of leisure by the look of it.
Roma Oh no, I think she works.

Jennifer stretches her arms and legs as:

Michael Well her arms and legs move, I don't know about the rest of her.

He enjoys his joke

Roma With her husband, I mean. What d'you think then?
Michael No, anyway, it's fancy dress.
Roma They don't have to wear fancy dress.

Michael looks into the boxes, tapping them and so on as:

Michael Well I tell you this, Roma—they'd better. We've gone to a great deal of effort
Roma Yes, but Mickey . . .
Michael Why are you so anxious?
Roma Anxious?
Michael Anxious—about them.
Roma Not *anxious*, Mickey. (*She smiles gaily to show how unanxious she is*)
Michael I take your point about PR but some other time—not tonight. It'll be crowded enough as it is. Besides which, it'll mess up our numbers—the food and so on. Now then—stereo.

Michael goes inside

Roma stands for a moment, looking decidedly anxious and does some of her calming deep breathing

Roma follows him inside as:

Mrs Hinson comes out of her kitchen

Mrs Hinson Now then, who's for a refreshing beverage?
Jennifer Not for me, thanks, Mum. (*She stands*) David tells me you'll be coming back with us.
Mrs Hinson You won't mind that, will you, dear?
Jennifer Mind? Why should I mind?
Mrs Hinson (*leaning heavily on the frame*) Have a feel if my pinny's getting dry, will you, Jennifer?
Jennifer (*with a false smile*) You're surely not thinking of bringing it with you —not just for one night?

She feels the pinny, unpegs it and gives it to Mrs Hinson

Mrs Hinson Well I certainly needed it the last time I came, didn't I, dear? I could have grown radishes in the dust under your furniture—and how you can find anything in that airing cupboard of yours.
Jennifer How do you manage and you with your hip and that terrible migraine?

Mrs Hinson You know me, dear, if there's plenty to be done, I'm the one to be doing it.

They "smile" at each other

David comes out as:

Any old how, much as I enjoy your company I can't stand here chit-chatting all day.

Jennifer (*insincerely*) Is there anything I can do?

Mrs Hinson No thank you, dear, I'm just going to give my pinny a quick iron —you sit down before you fall down, there's a lot of it about.

Mrs Hinson goes inside

Jennifer One night—yes. Two nights—possibly. More than that—forget it.

David Don't go getting yourself worked up again.

Jennifer I don't want her staying with us.

David Why do you get so worked up?

Jennifer Because the last time she stayed with us, we didn't speak for the next two weeks and I don't think that's healthy.

David I spoke, you threw things.

Jennifer I can't stand seeing what happens to you when *she's* around.

David Jen, she stays with us twice a year, at the most.

Jennifer And both times she stays four months, at the least.

David That isn't true, it only feels like four months.

Jennifer It feels like ten months and there's no "only" about it.

He makes to touch her

I mean it, David. I'm being unreasonable and I know I'm being unreasonable but I can't bear the thought of her, in my house, running around in her stupid bloody pinny, stuffing you full of tinned fruit and her rotten rice pudding—does she know you're forty years old?

David She's my mother. I'm her only son. I can't ignore her.

There is a moment between them

Just—sit down—enjoy the sun—and take it easy.

Jennifer You really think I can enjoy sitting here surrounded by her knickers. (*She flutters one of the items on the line*)

David Pretend you're on a yacht.

David goes into the kitchen

Jennifer stands for a moment, then takes up her handbag and defiantly lights a cigarette. She sits smoking as:

Michael backs out of the french windows, hunched over a JBL speaker

Michael Make sure the wires are tight against the wall, okay, I don't want people tripping over them and ruining the equipment.

Michael backs along the house wall, keeping the wire tight against it. He sets down the speaker and stands back to survey its position

He hurries inside again as:

Roma comes out, holding the telephone

Roma (*clearly intent on saying something*) Mike . . .

But Michael is far too intent on setting up the equipment

The telephone rings, causing her to jump

Michael backs out the french windows with a second speaker

Roma goes inside to answer the telephone

Michael The position of the speakers is—very important—far more important than people—realise. Critical in fact. Most people wouldn't bother—not for a do like—this—*but*—(*he stands back to check the position of the speakers*) if we don't get it right, we don't get the proper—stereo—separation. (*He moves to make a small adjustment to one of the speakers*) Okay?

No reply

Okay Ro?

Roma appears in the french windows, nursing the telephone

Roma (*vaguely*) Sorry.
Michael Now then, the way I see it is this—who was that?
Roma Wrong number.

Michael guides her to stand centrally DS

Michael Right, if you could stand here. No—as you were. Just about—here. Okay?

Michael hurries inside and out of sight

Roma remains, not moving

(*Off; loudly through a microphone*) Testing testing one two three, testing. (*Without the mike; calling*) Okay?
Roma (*more to herself*) As far as I know, how do I know, what do I know?
Michael (*loudly; through the microphone*) Can't hear. Okay?
Roma (*suddenly shouting violently; jumping up and down*) Okay! Okay, okay, okay, okay, okay!

At the sound of Roma's voice, Jennifer moves to peer through the hole in the fence but moves away as:

Michael appears in the french windows

Michael (*puzzled*) Okay?
Roma Sorry.
Michael I mean—you know—okay?

Roma Okay.

Michael Okay, we'll run through it again, okay? (*He starts to go inside*)

Roma Mike, I wonder if it might not be better for *you* to check—I mean your ear is so much better, anyway.

Michael looks at her for a moment

Michael Okay—it's all set up, all you have to do is press the play switch, nothing else, just the play switch.

Roma nods and goes inside

Michael takes up the central position. But, on second thoughts, he goes to the fence and peers over

Sorry about that. (*As a comical afterthought*) Thought we'd found the buried treasure and became rather over-excited. Sorry. (*He goes back to his position*)

Jennifer Found the what??

Jennifer moves to the fence and is about to say something to Michael when:

Roma comes out

Roma It doesn't work.

Michael Doesn't work?

Roma It doesn't seem to go.

Michael (*anxiously moving past her*) What d'you mean, it doesn't work, it must work.

Roma I pressed the switch and nothing happens.

Michael exits

(*Plucking up the courage to admit*) Mickey, I told a fib when I said that was a wrong number just now . . .

Michael comes out

Michael Someone has pressed the pause button.

Roma Oh.

Michael Not to worry, we'll try again, okay?

Michael pats Roma's bottom to send her on her way

Roma goes inside

Michael takes up his position DS

Michael Okay. Ready when you are.

There is a moment then music thunders through the speakers, perhaps Dire Straits. Whatever it is it is far too loud and distorted

Jennifer reacts as:

Michael hurries into the house as:

Roma appears in the french windows. A moment later the music stops blaring

David comes out of the kitchen

David Will you please stop following me around with a trayful of bloody food.

Mrs Hinson appears in the kitchen door with a tray bearing a jug, a dessert plate and spoon

Mrs Hinson Don't be so argumentative.

David unwillingly takes the tray and puts it on the table and sits as:

Mrs Hinson comes out, using the frame as:

Michael comes out of the french windows

Mrs Hinson You're just like your father—get a meal ready and there he was —gone.
Michael (*over the fence*) Sorry about that.
David There is more to life than Meals On Wheels. Right, Michael?
Michael (*smiling*) Right!

Michael goes indoors

Jennifer He's on a diet.
Mrs Hinson (*thrusting the plate at him*) Eat. (*To Jennifer*) He was looking a bit faint so I knocked him up a quick custard—you don't mind, do you, dear?
Jennifer (*hugely insincere*) Of course I don't mind. (*She bends to look at the food*) Mmmm, tinned pears—lovely!
Mrs Hinson They cost me nearly sixty-five pence but what does it matter when it's for someone you love?

Mrs Hinson nudges David

Come on—put some of that custard on—you love my custard.

David tips the jug to reveal the solid unshifting mass of custard

David When I can dislodge it.
Mrs Hinson You know it won't leave the jug on its own. It's the goodness in it. Use your spoon and ease it out.

Mrs Hinson goes into the kitchen

David tips out a solid lump of custard

David What am I supposed to do with this lot?
Jennifer (*beaming*) Eat.

Jennifer goes in through the french windows as:

Michael comes out of his french windows and takes up his central position

Michael (*calling*) Ready when you are and remember, just the play switch okay?

But Roma appears in the french windows, holding the telephone

Roma That wasn't a wrong number just now. It was Celia.
Michael Why didn't you say?
Roma You were busy.
Michael Well what did she want?
Roma They can't come because they've had a flood in their basement.
Michael I didn't know they *had* a basement.
Roma Neither did I. Apparently they've had one fitted.

The telephone rings

Roma jumps but this time she thrusts it into his hand

Please will you answer it, Michael.

Roma hurries in through the french windows

Michael Ro? (*He answers the telephone*) Hallo? What? Who *is* this?

Michael goes in through the french windows as:

Roma comes out of the kitchen with a biscuit. She goes DS *to the end of the shed, out of his sight, and neurotically nibbles at the biscuit as:*

Mrs Hinson backs out through the kitchen door, dragging a very large old suitcase

David (*moving quickly to her*) What are you *doing*?
Mrs Hinson What does it look like, I'm giving my case an airing.

Jennifer appears, stone-faced, in the french windows

Jennifer (*flatly*) What's this?
Mrs Hinson It's my case.
David This isn't the one you asked me to get out.
Jennifer Why—such—a big—case?
Mrs Hinson Well, if I'm going to stay for a few weeks, I'll need my bits and pieces, won't I, Jennifer?
Jennifer (*smiling humourlessly*) I see. (*She sits, inwardly raging*)
David (*to Mrs Hinson*) What d'you mean, a few weeks? Who said anything about a few weeks?
Mrs Hinson (*all innocence*) I thought *you* did.
David No! (*To Jennifer*) No!
Mrs Hinson Open this lid and get the mothballs out for me, David, there's a good boy.

He snatches the case from her

David Why do you do it? Why?

David goes inside with the case

Mrs Hinson (*knowing perfectly well*) What's he on about now?
Jennifer (*to herself, determined to remain calm*) It's not just me you do it to, it's him.
Mrs Hinson Par-don?

Jennifer (*standing; brightly*) All set then, are we? All ready for the big trek west?

Mrs Hinson feels her washing

Mrs Hinson There's no rush, is there, dear? Besides, I've got to wait for his pudding to cook.

Jennifer You're absolutely right. I'd quite forgotten about his pudding.

Jennifer goes inside

David closes the french windows. Throughout the following Jennifer and David can be seen having a "discussion" through the french windows

Michael comes out through the french windows

Michael That was Gareth.

Roma (*hopefully*) He and Sandy have patched it up and they're coming—super!

Michael No—they've had one of their rows.

Roma But he's already told us.

Michael He'd forgotten. He was drunk.

Michael goes to the shed and disappears inside

Roma Jeremy and Pat aren't coming either. They phoned when you were out. He's broken his arm, or she's broken his neck, I can't remember. That's Nick and Gilly and George and Di and Ivor and Henrietta and Jerry and Angela and Clive and Celia and Gareth and Sandy and the meat is still frozen and frankly, Mickey—frankly I'm beginning to wonder if this party is really such a good idea.

Roma takes up the box of chops as:

Michael comes out of the shed, vaguely aware that she has been saying something

Michael Sorry?

Roma No-one. I mean—nothing.

Michael I've had an idea about the cheese.

Roma I've had an idea about the chops.

Roma goes inside with the box of chops

Michael That's more like it. (*Calling after her*) The team!

Michael goes back into the shed, pleased with himself as:

David and Jennifer come out

David Off we go then, Mum, okay?

Mrs Hinson I say—David—aren't you supposed to be having your children this weekend?

David Next weekend. Right, let's get your case packed.

Mrs Hinson Put the iron on for me, there's a good boy, I still haven't done my pinny.

He grits his teeth, but maintains the peace and goes back inside

Mrs Hinson He misses his children dreadful you know.
Jennifer Yes, I *do* know.
Mrs Hinson Poor little mites. Still, takes all sorts, doesn't it, dear?
Jennifer It does indeed.
Mrs Hinson Mind you, she's a good mother, that Rosemary, for all her abnormal characteristics. (*Groping in her handbag*) Oh yes, I've got those snaps I was telling you about. That house we all took in Bournemouth that summer. That was a lovely holiday that was. Oh yes, the children were so happy—well, they love being with their father. That was in the August, just prior to him meeting you in the September and deserting them in the October . . .
Jennifer (*politely*) Excuse me, I suddenly feel quite sick.

Jennifer goes into the kitchen, brushing past David who was on his way out into the garden

David turns to look at her

There is a pause. Then a door slams and Jennifer lets out a great yell of pent-up fury

David looks at his mother who sits, her back to him

David hurries inside

Mrs Hinson (*smugly*) I think she's on the turn myself. (*She sits, happily contemplating the havoc she has caused*)

Michael comes out of the shed with a large handsaw and a workmate bench which he sets up.

He takes the block of cheese and clamps it onto the bench. He is just about to saw a slice off it when:

Roma opens an upstairs bedroom window and leans out, holding the box of chops, and lets the box fall where it lands with a crash. She immediately closes the window

Michael freezes, turns, and looks at the box. He reaches in to take out a fistful of shattered chops which he lets run through his fingers. He looks up at the bedroom window

Michael (*puzzled*) Roma . . . ?

Michael goes in through the kitchen door

Jennifer appears behind the french windows. She glares at Mrs Hinson's back. Then she opens the doors quietly and stands behind Mrs Hinson. She suddenly does a lady-like V-sign, then a huge, exaggerated V-sign with both hands. Then she sticks her tongue out at her and puts her fingers to her nose etc. like a ten year old, totally abandoned

Mrs Hinson remains totally unaware

Jennifer sees the walking frame. She takes it up as though to hurl it at Mrs Hinson. Then she has a wonderful idea. She tiptoes to the fence and throws the frame into the Smethurst garden. As soon as she does so she is overcome with guilt. The guilt rapidly turns to laughter

Roma comes out of the french windows and moves DS *with her back to the house, where she performs her deep breathing exercises*

Michael comes out of the kitchen, holding pieces of chop, still looking for some explanation. He is about to demand one of Roma, when he sees the walking frame. He stares at it

Mrs Hinson looks at Jennifer

Jennifer tries to stop laughing but it only becomes more manic

David comes out of the kitchen and stares at her

Jennifer goes in through the french windows, pulling them closed so that we can see but not hear her laughing

Mrs Hinson (*contentedly*) Oh yes. On the turn she is—definitely . . .

David stares through the window at Jennifer who is hopelessly trying to stifle her manic laughter

Mrs Hinson, unaware of all this, takes up her "TV Times" as——

——*the* CURTAIN *falls*

ACT II

The same. Seven fifteen, the same evening. It is still light

Both sets of french windows are open

The chairs and the washing are still out in the Hinson garden

The Smethurst garden has been arranged for the party. The two tables, with matching cloths, have been set up. One is arranged along the fence and is for food—with various bowls of salad etc. covered in clingfilm. The second table, R, is for drinks. It holds the carton of wine, three bottles of lemonade and cider, six cans of beer and plastic glasses. Near it, there is a swing-lid bin. There are three or four various chairs, ex-skip and heavily-renovated. One of them is canvas with arms. Illuminated fairy lights arranged along the trellis at the back of the house. They flash dimly. The walking frame is US of the food table, near the fence

Loud pop music is coming from the speakers

Smoke is coming from behind the shed and drifting across towards the Hinson garden

After a moment, Roma comes out of the kitchen carrying a bowl of salad. She is wearing a white tie and tails that fit where they touch. Her flat patent shoes make her appear even dumpier. She does an elaborate ballroom step across to deposit the bowl on the table, singing as she goes. We cannot hear the words because of the volume of the music. She dances her way back into the kitchen and out again with paper plates and serviettes

As she sets them on the table, the music stops. She carries on singing until she gets to the end of the song—which is "Some Enchanted Evening" and has nothing to do with the music from the speakers

From behind the shed come metallic clunks and subdued curses. The smoke thickens

Roma closes the french windows, peers briefly over the fence, and then goes inside the kitchen as:

> *Michael backs out from behind the shed, coughing and waving a barbecue tool at the smoke. He wears a long wig, a bare-shouldered evening gown which is too short for him so that we glimpse his short socks and trainers. He also wears a small plastic apron and yellow kitchen gloves*

Michael (*as he backs out*) Roma!

Roma comes out of the kitchen carrying some plastic cutlery

Roma (*positively overbright*) Yes, Mickey.

Michael What's happened to the music?

Roma (*carrying the cutlery to the food table*) It stopped.

Michael The thing is—don't touch it. I'll do it as soon as I've got the barbecue under control. No, as you were—we'll leave it off until people actually arrive.

There is a puff of thicker smoke

Michael waves his way through the smoke to have a look at the problem

Roma There does seem to be an awful lot of smoke.

Michael waves his way back to her

Michael And you know why, don't you! That charcoal you bought was damp. Damp!

Roma (*opening her mouth to say something, but changing it to*) I was thinking about next door.

Michael Have a word. Any problems and you might mention that it's hardly the done thing to hang washing out on a Saturday. Oh, and you'd better say something about this thing. (*He indicates the walking frame*)

Michael waves his way back behind the shed

Roma Mickey, I'd rather you said something, you know how I hate . . .

Mrs Hinson comes out of her kitchen, sniffing the air. She makes much of waving away the smoke

Mrs Hinson Well that's charming, that is.

Roma moves to the fence

(*Moving nearer the fence; shouting*) I say that's charming, that is!

Roma jumps at the sound of her voice. She stands on tiptoe but is too short to see over the fence

Roma (*waving an arm*) Hello? I say—excuse me . . .

Mrs Hinson turns away to take the washing from the line

Roma gives up and goes into the kitchen as:

David comes out through the french windows. Seeing the smoke, he closes the windows as:

Roma comes out of the kitchen with the steps which she sets up near the fence as:

David helps his mother take down the washing which she folds into his arms

Mrs Hinson Lighting a bonfire on a Saturday.

David No, I think he's having trouble getting his barbecue started.

Mrs Hinson Ought to be ashamed of himself.

Roma mounts the steps

(*Shouting over her shoulder*) I say you ought to be ashamed of yourself!

Roma thinks better of trying to communicate. She returns the steps to the kitchen as:

David Come on Mum.
Mrs Hinson "Come on Mum", what?
David Time for us to go.
Mrs Hinson (*for the umpteenth time*) I've got things to *do*.
David You've been doing things for the past hour and a half.
Mrs Hinson I am not being rushed. Just a minute——

She staggers, supporting herself on his arm

Where's my frame?
David Where did you leave it?
Mrs Hinson It's gone.
David How d'you mean, "gone"?
Mrs Hinson Gone.
David When did you last use it?
Mrs Hinson How do I know?
David Well if you can't remember the last time you used it, it goes to show how much you need it, doesn't it?
Mrs Hinson Oh yes, that's very clever, that is—and whether I need it or not, my son, a walking frame does not get up on its hind legs and walk.
David What are you trying to say?
Mrs Hinson I'm saying that any person who is capable of kicking a hole in my cleaning bucket last time I tried to be helpful, is just as capable of taking it out on my walking frame.
David You think Jen's done something with it? Don't be daft.
Mrs Hinson Well, I wouldn't put it past her. She can be very violent at times.
David She gets upset.
Mrs Hinson Your Aunt Florrie used to get upset. It depended where the moon was.
David What's more, you deliberately upset her.
Mrs Hinson If you're looking to cast aspersions, my son, I suggest you cross-examine her hormones.

They move towards the kitchen, with her leaning heavily on his arm as:

David It'll be in the house somewhere.
Mrs Hinson (*insisting*) I had it out here. Where is she, anyway?
David The name is Jennifer and she's on the phone.
Mrs Hinson She's never off the phone, she must cost you a fortune.
David She's phoning for *me*—it's business.
Mrs Hinson Oh yes? (*She gives a derisive little jerk of the head*)
David I don't think you realise just how much she takes off my plate.
Mrs Hinson Well she certainly doesn't put much *on* it.

David and Mrs Hinson go into the kitchen as:

Roma comes out of her kitchen, secretly holding a small piece of food. Seeing that the garden is empty, she is about to pop it into her mouth when:

Michael backs out from behind the shed

Roma quickly puts the food into the swing-lid bin

Roma How's it coming?
Michael Well, it's going.
Roma Well done, Brown Owl. (*She takes the wine bottles out of the carton and puts them on the table*)

Michael re-arranges them regimentally and during the following puts the carton under the table

Michael Did you have a word?
Roma Umm, not yet—I mean, what do I say?
Michael You say—excuse me, is this yours?
Roma Yes, but suggesting they've thrown a walking frame over the fence. People don't do that sort of thing.
Michael People don't throw pork chops out of the bedroom window.
Roma Unfair Mickey and you know it.
Michael (*advancing on her*) Do they . . .! Do they . . .?
Roma You know perfectly well I had a reason!
Michael And so—might—they——

He suddenly pounces at her in an attempt to tickle her. Roma takes up the walking frame to defend herself

Michael Yes or no—yes or no?
Roma Unfair, unfair. (*She giggles*)

There is the feeling that, as before they are going through the motions of having fun, rather than actually having it

David comes out of the french windows. He hears the sounds from next door and peeps through the spyhole

He watches Roma and Michael fighting over his mother's walking frame

David reacts, puzzled, takes another look and then goes back inside

Michael Yes or no? Admit—admit . . .
Roma Yes, yes, yes all right, all right Mister Nasty you win.
Michael Prize. (*He purses his lips*)
Roma Oh, honestly.

Roma puts down the frame and pertly kisses him on the lips. He takes her in his arms and dances with her

Michael D'you know—I'm really looking forward to this evening. What's the time? Twenty five past. Another half an hour and this place will be bursting.
Roma (*beaming*) Yes.
Michael We're going to have a lot of fun, really let our hair down.

Roma (*with a bright idea*) I know, let's have a drink.
Michael Now?
Roma Yes.
Michael Before people arrive?
Roma Yes.
Michael You mean a drink drink?
Roma *Yes*.
Michael All right, we'll have a drink. (*He opens a bottle and pours two rather small measures of white wine*)

Roma practices dancing, using the walking frame as a partner, during the following

Roma The thing is of course, *I* should lead. Later on—when we dance—being the man.
Michael You will be wearing your hat, won't you?
Roma Oh yes. That's my favourite bit, the hat.
Michael Because the thing about Fred Astaire, surely, was the top hat.
Roma I don't think he wore it all the time though. Any more than Ginger Rogers wore rubber gloves and a pinny.
Michael What I mean is—as long as we're ready for inspection when they arrive.
Roma (*gaily*) If they arrive . . .
Michael Ro.
Roma Sorry.
Michael All right, a few people have cancelled. It's unfortunate but it's not going to spoil our evening. Is it?
Roma No of course it isn't.

She takes a glass from him

Thank you darling.
Michael Cheers.
Roma (*toasting the house*) Happy happy home. Mmm—lovely.

They kiss briefly

Michael (*immediately*) We haven't done the ashtrays.
Roma I was just about to.
Michael Do we really think that three out here is enough? You know what they're like, some of these people . . .
Roma We did say three. Three out here, three inside.
Michael As long as we keep an eye on them. Anything *al fresco* and people flick—willy-nilly.

Michael goes behind the shed

Roma sneaks another small shot of wine

She goes into the kitchen as:

David and Jennifer come out of the french windows

Jennifer Where?

David (*indicating over the fence*) There.
Jennifer Well?
David Well did you or didn't you?
Jennifer No.
David Jen . . .
Jennifer Oh all right, yes I did.
David Why?
Jennifer I don't know why. Yes I do—because she drives me crazy.
David Great.
Jennifer No it isn't, it's pathetic.

Mrs Hinson appears in the french windows

Mrs Hinson I say, David, I can't get my television on.
David What d'you mean, can't get it on?
Mrs Hinson I switch it on and nothing happens.
Jennifer (*beaming*) You can watch *our* television.
Mrs Hinson I can't go *now*.
David What d'you mean, you can't go now?
Mrs Hinson If I go now I shall miss my programme and I'm sure not even you
     would wish that on me, Jennifer.
David What programme?
Mrs Hinson My quiz programme. It's the All Area Golden Final. God alone
     knows I don't get many pleasures since your poor dear father . . .
David What time does it start?
Mrs Hinson Half past.

Jennifer moves away, knowing the outcome

David Okay, fine, watch your programme and then we're going straight
     home, okay? Straight home.

David looks at Jennifer who regards him stonily

Mrs Hinson Yes all right, Son. (*She gives him a brief peck. Instantly*) If you
     can get it started.

David goes in through the french windows

Jennifer sits in the deckchair and reaches for her handbag

Mrs Hinson That's right, dear—you have a nice read of your credit cards
     while I assist my David.

Mrs Hinson goes inside

Jennifer takes out a cigarette and lights it as:

Roma comes out of the kitchen with three ashtrays which she distributes as:

Michael backs out from behind the shed

Roma In fact I think we should make it a rule.
Michael Rule?
Roma Girls, stroke boys, lead—in the dancing.

Michael Oh, yes. Yes.

Roma That should be really good fun.

Michael That's what we want—fun. Just a minute—these lights are on. (*He points to the fairy lights*)

Roma They're supposed to be on, surely?

Michael Not now, Ro—when it's dark. (*He points to one of the ashtrays*) Not this one I don't think, this one is rather good.

Michael goes into the kitchen and the fairy lights go out. He comes out again

We're not paupers but there's no point in throwing it away.

He goes behind the shed

Roma stands, chastened, then she takes the "good" ashtray into the kitchen as:

David comes out of the french windows

David I dunno what's wrong with it.

Mrs Hinson comes out after him

Mrs Hinson Your Rosemary was good with televisions, I seem to remember. What she used to do was twiddle with those knobs at the back.

David (*patiently*) It doesn't work.

Mrs Hinson Can't you phone the engineer?

Jennifer Or Rosemary—why don't you phone Rosemary, darling?

Roma comes out with a replacement ashtray. She positions it, and goes back inside

David It's no good—the tube must have gone.

Mrs Hinson Well can't you find another one?

David (*for the first time, a glimpse of his patience fraying*) No. No, I can't.

Mrs Hinson Well it's no good you standing there popping your eyes out at me—look at the time.

David You'll just have to miss it for once, won't you?

Jennifer (*cupping her hand to her ear*) Do I hear the distant rumble of minor insurrection?

Mrs Hinson I knew we should have gone earlier. Hanging about—making me miss my programme. (*She sulkily takes up her "TV Times"*)

Jennifer Well it *is* the All Area Golden Final and what about Kay and John?

David (*to Mrs Hinson*) Are you coming or aren't you?

Mrs Hinson (*with her nose in her magazine*) Ordering me about—I'm not one of your shopgirls, you know.

David No. No, you're not. (*He looks at them and can't resist*) Thirty-two people I employ. Thirty-two smiling contented people who think the sun shines out of my profit gland. But you two—(*to Jennifer*) you're right. I'm weak and I'm useless and I give up. *You* get her to move—I'm going for a walk.

David goes inside

Jennifer and Mrs Hinson sit in silence

The front door slams

There is a pause

Mrs Hinson Walking about, this time of night, he'll get himself mugged.
Jennifer He won't go far: down to the corner for some cigars I should think.
It's about as far as the cord will stretch. (*She "beams" at Mrs Hinson and
takes up her handbag*)

Jennifer goes inside

Mrs Hinson sits, moodily flicking through her magazine as:

*Michael comes out from behind the shed, with his wig in his hand to mop his
brow*

Roma appears excitedly in the french windows

Roma Toby's here!
Michael Where?
Roma He's parking the car.

The Smethurst doorbell rings

Mrs Hinson Door!

Roma hurries back inside

Michael (*shouting after her*) Hat! Hat! (*He quickly puts on his wig, using the
window as a mirror, then realises he is still wearing the pinny and gloves. He
pulls them off and shoves them behind the shed*)

Toby (*off*) Oh I see, Fred Astaire, very good.

Toby and Roma come through the french windows

*Toby is about the same age as Michael, very tall and slim. He wears an
immaculate white suit, white shoes and socks, red buttonhole and a completely
incongruous red fez*

Roma now wears a top hat and carries a wrapped bottle of wine

Don't tell me I'm the first?
Roma It's lovely to see you . . .
Toby (*seeing the food on the table*) And it's a barbecue, eh? (*He rubs his hands
together enthusiastically*) Great—I'm starving.
Roma Look darling—Toby's brought a bottle of wine. (*She unwraps the
wine, puting the paper in the bin and the bottle on the table*)
Toby Well now, if Roma is Fred Astaire, you must be—no—give up.
Michael Ginger—Rogers.
Toby With a moustache. Very good.

*During the following Roma takes off her hat. She puts it on the table and adjusts
her hair*

Michael And you?

Toby (*posing*) The Man In The White Suit. There was a film. You remember.

Michael (*disdainfully, of the fez*) What about that thing?

Toby Well I had it in the cupboard so I thought I'd throw it in as a sort of bonus. Some lucky girl gets *me* and the hat. (*He poses*) Olé.

Michael You do know there's a theme, do you? Famous Couples in Reverse.

Toby Ah—yes—true—but travelling solo, I couldn't see much point.

Roma I thought you were bringing Caroline.

Toby I was. Her husband came back from Zimbabwe or she had to wash her hair, something like that, I can't remember. (*He sees the walking frame, frowns at it, then pulls out a packet of cigarettes*) Anyway, I have to tell you that I'm really looking forward to this evening.

Roma Yes, it'll be fun.

Michael Watch the shrub, will you?

Toby Sorry?

Michael (*indicating*) You're leaning on the shrub.

Toby lights his cigarette with a match

Roma "discreetly" holds out an ashtray

Toby deposits the match in the ashtray

The Smethurst doorbell rings

Mrs Hinson Door!

Roma (*gaily*) Who will this be, I wonder?

Roma makes to go inside

Michael Hat!

Roma hurries back to the table and puts on her hat

Roma hurries inside

Toby The thing is. I've got this feeling I'm really going to click tonight. I might even propose to someone. Suddenly feel the need to get married again, would you believe.

Michael Oh really? Now what was I going to ask you—ah yes—I want you to look after the stereo.

Toby Any chance of a drink first?

From inside the house comes a shriek. It is Sandy reacting to Roma's costume

Michael (*not over-generously*) Red or white?

Toby White always tastes better outdoors, don't you think? Yes, a glass of white.

Michael takes up one of his bottles

Actually, I brought a bottle of rather good Chablis.

Sandy comes through the french windows, followed by Roma

Sandy is about thirty and is extravagant in every way. She wears a striped rugby shirt belted over brief shorts to exaggerate her generous curves, striped socks and high heels. The shirt has the number sixty-nine on it. She carries a mobile telephone

From the moment Sandy arrives, Toby has eyes only for her

Sandy (*as she enters*) . . . I was coming as Gareth, d'you see, and he was coming as *me*—oh and a garden! And who do I see in it but Mister Michael Delicious Himself and looking an absolute dream in his new frock.

Sandy kisses Michael generously and gives him her phone

Put this somewhere for me, will you, cherub? Daren't leave it in the car . . . (*She turns her attention immediately to Toby*) And who is this divine little pixie?

Michael passes the telephone to Roma who puts down her hat

Roma Oh—yes—of course, you haven't met. This is Toby, Toby Hancock. Toby, this is Sandra—Sandy—Sandy Lloyd-Meredith.

Toby recovers, closing his mouth, pulling off his hat, and dropping his cigarette on the paving—to the horror of Roma and Michael. He extends his hand and crushes the cigarette underfoot at the same time

Toby How d'you do?

Sandy takes his hand and looks at him adoringly

Roma puts down the telephone

Roma Sandy's in property. (*She discreetly retrieves the crushed cigarette and puts it in an ashtray as:*)
Toby Oh—really? Great!!
Sandy And don't tell me—you're another one of these wonderful medical people.
Toby Anaesthetist, actually.
Sandy (*looking deep into his eyes*) God, I think you people are *wonderful*. Wonderful. All that—dedication and blood and everything. (*She holds the look and then suddenly shrieks*) *Oh my* god!

Mrs Hinson reacts to the shriek

Michael What's happened?
Sandy For one terrible moment I thought someone was thrusting a large drink into my hand

Mrs Hinson moves to the fence and looks through the peephole as:

Roma—worried about the neighbours—goes to the fence and peeps through the hole

So that for a moment, the two women are eyeball to eyeball

Mrs Hinson goes indoors

Sandy takes Toby's hand and guides him to the drinks table

Now then, what have we here . . . There's red wine and there's white wine which I suspect is Michael's homemade *vin de* stinging nettle *avec* turnip. Oh no it isn't, bad luck, and there's lemonade and designer shandy and oh look—medium dry cider—*mmmm*.

Toby Actually, I brought a bottle of rather good Chablis.

Sandy Now *that*, would be perfecto. (*She proffers a glass*)

There is an irritable blast on a van horn

Toby uncorks the bottle

Michael She didn't bring a bottle.

Roma No.

Michael Well say something.

Roma Mickey . . .

Michael I thought they weren't coming, anyway. (*He has an awful thought*) Just a minute—where's Gareth?

The Smethurst doorbell rings

Roma More guests!

Toby Great!

Roma makes to hurry to answer the door

Michael (*calling after her*) Hat!

Roma hurries back for the hat and makes to hurry out again, but Sandy takes her to one side

Sandy (*in a dramatic meaningful whisper*) If it's Gareth, I'm not here and it might be advisable not to let him in, all right darling?

Roma looks at Sandy

The Smethurst doorbell rings again

Roma hurries inside

Michael Actually, it was clearly indicated on the invitation . . .

Sandy Sorry, pussycat?

Michael It was on the invitation. N.B.P.B.A.B.

Sandy (*thinking briefly*) Give up.

Michael N.B. *Note Bene*. P.B.A.B. Please Bring A Bottle—N.B.P.B.A.B.

Sandy Well there you are, d'you see, I thought it was some terribly exclusive postcode.

Roma comes out of the house

Roma I wonder if you'd mind moving your car, Toby? Mr McMonagle's son has come back and they can't unload the Dormobile.

Michael Roma, will you please advise him to park that disgusting heap of his a little less flamboyantly.

Roma Yes, I know darling but it's just keeping the peace—d'you mind, Toby?

Toby Not at all. (*He smiles at Sandy to show her what a reasonable kind of guy he is*)

Toby goes inside

Roma takes off her hat

Sandy steps onto the rungs of the walking frame, raises her glass and toasts the house

Sandy Be good, house. (*To Roma and Michael*) Health and happiness and lots of everything.

Roma realises that they do not have a drink. She quickly takes up the two glasses they drank from earlier and gives one to Michael

Michael (*whispering*) Where's *Gareth*?

Roma I don't *know*, Mickey. (*She puts her hat on the table*)

Michael Well find out—I don't want any trouble.

Sandy knocks back her wine

Sandy What shall I do with this empty glass? No, don't worry, I've had an idea. (*She refills her glass*)

Michael Speak to her.

Roma Wouldn't it be better if *you* . . .

Michael Roma, I'm trying to re-activate the barbecue. That's right—the charcoal you bought has nearly gone out again.

Michael goes behind the shed

Sandy Has he got another woman behind there?

Roma Sorry? Oh—no—Michael? No, he's preparing the barbecue.

Sandy Yes of course, it's a *barbecue*. (*Calling to the unseen Michael*) Do let me know if I can prick a sausage or anything, darling! (*She finishes her drink*)

Roma Actually—(*she tries to make light of it*) we were wondering about Gareth.

Sandy (*dramatically*) I beg you—do not mention that man's name. (*She pours herself another drink*)

Roma Oh dear, you've been fighting again.

Sandy Let's just say it's been a terribly busy week and I hate him.

Michael hurries out from behind the shed, now wearing the pinny and gloves. He goes straight into the kitchen

(*Calling after him*) Love the accoutrements, Mickey. Harvey Nicks—right? All that energy. He doesn't change, does he?

Roma Not often—no.

Roma "laughs" but quickly shows her concern as:

Michael comes out of the kitchen with a large box of matches. Without looking at the women, he goes straight behind the shed

He's worked so hard for this evening. I know people think he can be very
. . . What's the word . . .?

Sandy clamps a hand over her mouth

Obsessive—and what worries me is that we've already had several
cancellations and quite frankly I was beginning to wonder—I mean,
Gareth said *you* weren't coming.

Sandy grabs Roma's arm dramatically

Sandy You mean he's phoned?
Roma Twice actually.
Sandy What exactly did he say?
Roma Well, the first time he said you weren't coming and the second time
Michael took the call and, well it wasn't too clear actually—we think he
was at the rugby club—he sounded rather—you know——
Sandy Pissed out of his skull.
Roma —although I did gather that you'd had one of your disagreements.
Sandy I've left him.
Roma Oh . . .
Sandy Walked out on him. (*She clicks her fingers indicating "just like that"*)
Roma When?
Sandy Lunch-time.
Roma Umm, you *did* say he doesn't know you're here, didn't you, Sandy? I
mean he can be awfully . . .
Sandy Good God darling, of course he doesn't know I'm here—unless
someone's told him—which I wouldn't put past *some* of our so-called
chums—I mean, can you *imagine* what he might do if he tracks me down?
The man's a *monster*. I mean incredibly attractive and wonderful between
the sheets but a *monster*. (*She shudders, but in anticipation rather than fear*)

She takes Roma's arm, who is transfixed

So you see, darling—one way and another I'm feeling incredibly low and
in desperate need of a good old-fashioned cuddle. (*She smiles wanly but
immediately recovers*) Oh my God, listen to me. Music! I need music! Why
isn't there any music?

Sandy goes in through the french windows

Roma, who has been transfixed, is suddenly galvanised into action

Roma No, no, I don't think you'd better touch Mickey's . . .

Michael comes out from behind the shed

Michael Well where is everyone? They're completely ruining my schedule.
Roma Mickey—about Gareth . . .

There is a sudden great blast of music from the speakers

Sandy comes out and starts gyrating wildly to the music

Michael remonstrates with Roma and she defends herself—neither they nor we can hear what is being said because of the noise

Mrs Hinson comes out of her kitchen with a broom and shouts soundless abuse over the fence as:

Sandy grabs Michael and tries to get him to dance

Michael extricates himself and hurries in through the french windows

Sandy dances in after him, followed by Roma as:

Mrs Hinson raises the broom and is just about to attack the fence when:

Jennifer comes out through the french windows and grabs the broom to stop her

A tug-a-war ensues—the broom becoming the symbol of their relationship

The music stops

Mrs Hinson and Jennifer's struggle stops

Mrs Hinson (*shouting*) I should think so an'all! I can't stay here, my nerves won't stand it. Where's he gone that boy?
Jennifer He'll have gone for a walk. He likes to go for a walk. It helps sort his mind out.
Mrs Hinson Oh yes?

Mrs Hinson puts the broom against the house wall as:

Sandy comes out of the french windows, with her hands up in a gesture of surrender

Sandy Sorry— sorry, sorry, sorry. (*She tiptoes exaggeratedly away*)

Michael closes the french windows, behind which he and Roma can be seen "discussing" things

Mrs Hinson We could have gone hours ago.
Jennifer We should have gone hours ago.
Mrs Hinson (*"en route" for the kitchen*) I cannot be rushed. And what is more —and as well you know, Jennifer—I cannot find my Zimmer.

Mrs Hinson goes into the kitchen

Jennifer glares after her, then turns and takes up the broom. She waves it over the fence

Jennifer Excuse me!

Sandy, who is about to pour herself a drink, turns to see the waving broom

Sandy Hello?

Both women move to the fence and raise up on their toes to look over it

Jennifer Sorry to disturb you. I wonder if you would be so kind as to return my mother-in-law's walking frame? (*She indicates the frame, making her request sound perfectly reasonable*)
Sandy This?
Jennifer Would you mind?
Sandy Not at all.

Sandy passes the frame over the fence

Jennifer Thank you so much. Enjoy your party.

Jennifer plonks the frame down as:

Mrs Hinson comes out of her kitchen

Mrs Hinson And I'll tell you something else—(*but she sees the frame*) where did this come from?

During the following Sandy listens at the fence and reacts dramatically

Jennifer Let's get one thing very clear. I can shout and scream and get things off my chest. He can't. And he doesn't—it all goes on inside.
Mrs Hinson (*stiffly*) I don't know what you're talking about, I'm sure.
Jennifer Oh I think you do.
Sandy Oh I think she does . . .

Jennifer plonks the frame in front of Mrs Hinson

Jennifer Mother . . .

Jennifer goes in through the french windows as:

Michael and Roma come out through their french windows

Roma (*gaily*) Sorry about that.
Michael The thing is, er, Sandy—Roma's been telling—me all this stuff about you and Gareth.
Roma (*trying to keep it light*) Not now, darling, it's a party.

The Smethurst doorbell rings

Mrs Hinson Door! (*She uses the frame to move and sit in her chair*)
Roma More guests!

Roma makes to hurry inside

Michael Hat!

Roma grabs her hat from the table

Sandy (*intercepting Roma; whispering*) If it's him, I'm not here okay?

Roma almost says something, but instead hurries in through the french windows

Sandy Now then Michael——

Sandy takes Michael's arm

(*Appearing to be serious*) Roma tells me you made that frock out of a pair of abandoned curtains. Is this true?

Michael No, it is not true. We hired.

Sandy (*aghast*) Hired? You mean it never came out of a skip?

Michael No—we hired. From Gaytime And Gala.

Roma, and Toby come out through the french windows, both wearing their hats

Toby Bit *aggressive*, isn't he?

Roma Yes, he and Mike have had one or two rather nasty little exchanges.

Toby (*to Michael*) I say the bloke across the road's a bit aggressive. (*He lights a cigarette*)

Roma indicates an ashtray

Michael He's a bloody idiot.

Sandy Mickey was telling me that you *hired* your costumes.

Roma We were hoping for something a little more political actually. We had in mind the Perons. Having seen the show and bought the CD. Unfortunately all they had in stock was this or—what was it again, Mickey?

Michael A spaceman or a giant banana.

Roma Which hardly fitted in with our theme—besides—(*she "laughs"*) can you imagine me as a spaceman and Mickey as a banana?

Toby Well since you mention it . . .

Sandy clamps a hand over his mouth

Michael Excuse me.

Michael goes behind the shed

Roma (*brightly*) Well now, where were we?

The doorbell rings

Mrs Hinson Door!

Roma More guests!

Toby Great!

Sandy Gareth! (*She dramatically mimes "don't let him in"*)

Roma makes to go inside as:

Michael puts his head round the shed

Michael Hat!

Roma hurries back and then realises that she is already wearing the hat, and hurries out through the french windows

Toby uses the window to check the rakish angle of his fez

Mrs Hinson I suppose it's going to be ring ring ring all night!

Mrs Hinson goes in through the french windows, leaving the frame outside

Sandy links arms with Toby

Sandy (*intimately*) I know you people hate talking shop, but you don't
   perchance know a decent therapist, do you? (*She looks meaningfully into
   his eyes*) My life is a mess, darling. A mess.
Toby Oh—well—look—if there's anything *I* can——
Sandy (*pressing a finger to his lips*) I'll tell you all about it later. Which
   reminds me—(*even more intimately*) you didn't happen to see a rather
   short but incredibly well-built Welsh person with mad eyes roaming the
   streets just now, did you?
Toby (*lightly*) No, why, should I have done?
Sandy (*dramatically*) God I hope not, darling, for all our sakes.

His smile freezes as she breaks away from him and tosses back a drink

Michael comes from behind the shed and takes Toby to one side

Michael Be very very careful—she's trouble.

Michael goes straight back behind the shed as:

Roma comes out, followed by David

Roma This is Mr Hinson from next door. Now then, this is Sandra Lloyd-
   Meredith who prefers to be called Sandy, and this is Toby, Toby Hancock.
David David Hinson—hello.

Michael comes out from behind the shed, looking decidedly harrassed

Roma Darling—Mr Hinson's here—from next door.
David (*raising a hand*) Hello again, Michael.
Michael Derek.
Roma David.
David (*pointing*) Love the frock.
Sandy (*catching his elbow*) Gaytime And Gala but you'll have to hurry.

Toby carelessly flicks ash on the paving

Roma sees it and looks fearfully at Michael who hasn't seen it

David Bonnie Langford, right? Bonnie Langford and Ken Livingstone.
Roma Fred Astaire and Ginger Rogers actually.
David Sorry.
Sandy (*squeezing his arm*) Darling—it could have been Dan Dare and a
   banana.
Michael D'you mind? Sorry.
David Do I mind what?
Michael You're leaning on the shrub.
David The what—sorry?

Michael points behind David

Michael The *Santolina Neapolitana.*

Roma (*changing the subject quickly*) Mr Hinson has come to collect his mother's—(*she sees the frame has gone*) oh. Has anyone seen a—(*she demonstrates*) walking frame?

Michael Excuse me—work to do. And do be careful of the vegetation. Thank you.

Michael strides purposefully behind the shed

Sandy I gave it back to the woman next door. She asked me for it about, oh, five minutes ago.

Sandy, Roma, David and Toby look over the fence to see the frame parked outside the house

David (*giving an open-handed gesture of apology*) Sorry to break up the fun.

Sandy (*intimately*) Darling, it could be the highlight of the entire evening.

David Anyway, you're probably wondering how it got over here?

Roma (*lightly*) Well we did er . . . .

David It's those magpies.

Sandy You mean a magpie tore it away from your poor mother—how terribly Hitchkovian.

David More your Rossini really. There's a surfeit of magpies, right?

Roma Is there?

David (*unwrapping a fresh pack of cigars; delivered with massive authority*) Certainly. Now they may look the business but they're little rascals—stealing eggs out of other nests, dive-bombing defenceless babies—general vandalism of that nature.

Toby, Roma and Sandy are transfixed

Anyway, this afternoon there's this pair of magpies behaving in a typically anti-social fashion and my wife—who is heavily into saving the whale etcetera—threw the nearest thing to hand at them—which happens to be my mother's Zimmer—only of course the magpies fly away and the Zimmer flies over the fence—hence my knocking on your door and disturbing the frivolities.

Sandy bursts into applause

Michael backs out from behind the shed

David offers Michael a cigar

Michael (*heavily*) We don't smoke. (*He hisses at Roma*) Where *is* everyone?

Michael goes into the kitchen

David Well I won't keep you good people any longer.

Roma (*quickly*) Why don't you join us for a drink?

David Ahh . . . (*He looks at his watch*)

Roma gives him an ashtray while at the same time relieving him of the cigar pack wrapping

Roma Unless you have a prior engagement.

David Well yes we did, but—er . . .

Behind Roma's back, Sandy is miming a plea of, "Please, please . . .!"

Yes, that would be very nice, thank you.
Roma (*pointedly*) And your wife of course. (*She hands David a can of drink*)
David She'd like that—yes, I'll umm . . . (*He peers over the fence*)
Roma (*beaming at Sandy and Toby*) The more the merrier.

Toby—who is somewhat miffed at no longer having Sandy all to himself—moodily flicks ash on the shrub

Roma audibly catches her breath. She "discreetly" passes an ashtray to him

David Ah—she's not there. I'll just umm . . . (*He indicates to "go round"*)

Sandy picks up her mobile phone and holds it out to him

Sandy (*gazing into his eyes*) No, don't go—not now you're here—give her a little tinkle.
David Oh—yes—right—thanks.
Sandy We'll leave you to it then. (*To Toby*) Come along, cherub.

Sandy guides Toby in through the french windows

Roma looks anxiously after them

David (*lightly; dialling*) Course if I'd *known*, I'd have slipped into something a bit more suitable.

Roma looks at him, not understanding, more concerned about what Sandy and Toby might be up to

Fancy dress.
Roma (*dawning*) Oh—yes—well I think I might just possibly have a little something, actually.

David's mobile phone on the Hinson table starts to ring

Instantly, Mrs Hinson's head comes round the french windows

Mrs Hinson Phone!

Mrs Hinson goes out of sight again immediately

Roma beams and hurries inside as:

Jennifer comes out of the kitchen

Jennifer (*picking up the phone*) Hello?
David Jen?
Jennifer Where are you?
David Over here. (*He moves to the fence*)
Jennifer Over where?
David Here.
Jennifer (*looking over at him*) What are you doing over there?

Jennifer realises that she is still speaking into the phone, and turns it off and speaks to him direct. As does David

David (*indicating the frame*) I came to get that thing.
Jennifer Oh . . .
David What's happened with Kay and John?
Jennifer I cancelled—why?
David They've asked us in for a drink.
Jennifer I thought we were going home.
David No hurry, is there? Not now——
Jennifer (*not heavily*) No, I'm not in the mood—really.
David I've already said yes.
Jennifer Tell them I've got a headache or something.
David All right—I'll just have a quickie and do a bit of PR for the old lady.
  What's she doing?
Jennifer As far as I can make out, trying to give the television the kiss of life.
David Ten minutes at the most. Jen—I'm sorry.
Jennifer So am I.

They touch hands briefly over the fence

Jennifer goes inside, putting the telephone back on the table

David puts the telephone down, and gets himself a can of beer and sits

Michael comes out and stares in horror as:

David flicks cigar ash on a plant and tosses away the pull-ring of the can. On seeing Michael, David toasts him with the can

David Cheers then Michael. (*He drinks*)

Michael takes up the pull-ring and pointedly deposits it into the bin and puts an ashtray at David's elbow

Michael You're staying, are you?

Sandy and Toby come out into the garden, with her arm in his

Sandy How long have you been divorced?
Toby Oh—years.
Sandy What went wrong?
Toby Well, most men end up marrying their mothers—I ended up marrying
  my father.
Sandy Sweet, *sweet.*
David (*generally*) Last fancy dress party I went to, bloke turned up in a
  coffin.
Michael How can you turn up to a party in a coffin?
David They delivered him in a small lorry. Carried him through and propped
  him up in a corner on the patio.
Toby In a *coffin*?
David As I live and breathe.
Sandy What was he supposed to be?

David Dead I think. No-one had the nerve to ask him.

Michael Well if no-one asked him, perhaps he was. Didn't his eyes move or anything?

David Oh yes, quite often. Mind you, he never spoke. Just leaned there at a rakish thirty five degrees, knocking back gins and tonic and dropping peanuts all down his pyjamas. White silk they were—with a Union Jack embroidered on the pocket. Interesting touch that, I thought. "I Died For Britain" sort of thing. But—and this is the really creepy part—it was only after they'd carried him outside and loaded him back on the lorry that we realised that nobody actually knew him. Not the host, nobody. So, you never know, Michael, he could be here tonight.

There is a pause

Then Sandy applauds

Michael hurries back behind the shed as:

Roma hurries out through the french windows with her hands behind her back. She goes straight to David and produces a child's plastic policeman's helmet which she puts on his head, the elastic around his chin. David keeps this on throughout

Roma There, I knew the children had one somewhere.

Sandy (*intimately*) Darling, you look *so* attractive. (*Even more intimately*) I wonder if she's got a pair of handcuffs?

Roma (*beaming*) What about your wife?

David My wife. Ah—yes—she says to say thanks but—well, she's just come out of hospital as it happens and she's still a bit—you know . . .

Roma Oh dear, well if there's ever anything I can do . . .

Michael comes out from behind the shed

Michael (*announcing*) Look—no point beating about the bush—(*he checks, having seen David's hat*) I'm behind with the barbecue, okay? So I must ask you to bear with me and please—don't fiddle with the sound system of which you are I/C, okay Toby?

Michael goes back behind the shed

Toby I'm starving.

Roma Yes. (*Generally*) Do excuse me.

Roma follows Michael anxiously

David (*referring to next door*) I was born in that house.

Sandy Have you seen what they've done to this place? No? Then you shall have the Grand Tour.

Sandy links arms with David, guiding him in through the french windows

Toby is somewhat miffed at this

Sandy (*to Toby*) You too, and bring a bottle and some glasses, will you, cherub? (*She blows him a kiss*)

Sandy and David go inside

Toby grabs a bottle and three glasses and hurries in after them as:

Mrs Hinson comes out of her french windows

Jennifer follows her

Mrs Hinson (*shouting towards the fence*) Don't anyone ask *me* if I'd like a drink! I'm not the skivvie, you know!
Jennifer If you want to go—go.
Mrs Hinson I do not go where I am not welcome.
Jennifer Ah—but that's not strictly true, is it? (*She "smiles"*)

Jennifer goes inside

Mrs Hinson (*beadily*) I see.

Mrs Hinson takes up the frame and goes inside as:

Roma comes from behind the shed

Roma (*brightly*) Having fun, everyone? (*But her face drops when she sees that the garden is empty*) Hello?

Michael comes out with one of his announcements

Michael I should also like to draw your attention to—where are they?

There is a shriek from Sandy inside the house

Michael They're in the house! Roma, they're in the house! Why are they being allowed to roam around the house unattended? Will you please keep them all together—*out here*.

She squares up to him so that they will be toe to toe

Roma Excuse me but I am not a border collie besides which there are only three of them—three people, Michael.
Michael Then it should be easy for you, shouldn't it, and what about bloody *Gareth*?
Roma I don't *know* about "bloody Gareth", Michael, but I do know that I bought the charcoal where you told me to buy it because you'd done your comparative studies and that was the cheapest and we know why now, don't we?
Michael Where is the methylated spirits?
Roma In the shed.

They hold their glares

Michael goes behind the shed

(*Instantly repenting*) Do be careful with it, Mickey.

Roma follows him anxiously

Sandy, David and Toby come out of the french windows. Each has a drink, the two men are smoking, Toby holds the bottle of wine

David Are we the only ones coming to this party?

Toby I think they've invited quite a few, actually.

Sandy *Invited*, yes cherub, but are they going to *come*? I mean, would you?

Toby I have.

Sandy Most people managed to come up with an excuse—I mean, I'm only here because I feel sorry for Roma—not that I intend staying long . . .

David ⎫
Toby ⎭ *(together; a chorus of disappointment)* Oh.

Sandy I have to keep on the move, you see—there's a certain mad Welshman . . . .

Roma comes from behind the shed, fanning herself with her hat

Ah there you are, darling, I was just saying to these two gorgeous little pixies—isn't this house fun? I'm sure *you* think so.

Roma Oh yes, every night I go to bed and close my eyes and think "isn't this house fun?" and sometimes I can't stop laughing. (*She beams wildly at them and holds out an ashtray*)

David Well you've certainly made a few changes.

Roma That's Mickey though, isn't it? Once he's made up his mind to do something . . .

Sandy And when you think that most of it came out of a skip.

Roma Some of it anyway.

Sandy Michael is heavily into skips. If he sees an empty one being delivered, he'll follow it for miles.

Roma Rumour has it he found me on a skip, but it's not true.

Roma laughs gaily, expecting Sandy, David and Toby to join in but they don't

It really is quite extraordinary the things people throw away. These chairs for example. Recovered and then re-covered, you might say. And the tables, just thrown away. Of course, they needed attention but then, don't we all? We all need *some* attention, not much, but *some*, that's all—*some*.

The Smethurst doorbell rings

More guests! You see? More guests!

Toby Great!

Sandy (*"whispering" to Roma*) Gareth!

Michael comes out from behind the shed

Michael Hat!

Roma hurries inside, putting the hat on as:

Jennifer comes out into the garden

Sandy We've just been marvelling at the way you've done the entire house all by yourself, Mickey-boo.

Michael becomes even more smug than usual. He assumes that the others are transfixed by his wisdom. In fact, they are becoming increasingly aware of the thick pall of smoke that begins to rise from his wig

Michael The way I see it, it doesn't take too many 'A' Levels to saw a piece of wood in half or fix a bit of guttering. With the best will in the world, you can't say that the artisan class is over-endowed with the grey stuff.

Toby (*shouting*) Stand back!

Toby snatches the wig from Michael's head hurls it to the ground

David seizes the wig and hurls it over the fence

Jennifer sees it, quickly takes up the garden fork and tips the wig into the pond, using the fork to push it under

Michael, Toby, David and Jennifer hurry to line up and look over the fence, with Sandy on a chair as:

Roma comes out through the french windows with Mrs Hinson who is using the walking frame and has her handbag over her arm. She has taken off her pinny. She will very much play "the old lady"

Michael (*to Jennifer*) Do you mind? Thank you so much.

During the following Jennifer fishes the sodden wig out of the pond. Using the fork she puts it into the plastic bucket and holds it over the fence for Michael to take

Roma Look who's here, everyone! It's Mrs Hinson our nextdoor neighbour!

Sandy remains standing on the chair as they all turn to regard Mrs Hinson

David (*to Jennifer*) What's she doing here?

Mrs Hinson (*shyly*) How-do.

Roma (*putting her hat down*) Now then, who do you know? This is Sandra Lloyd-Meredith who prefers to be called Sandy. This is Toby, Toby Hancock, and this of course is my husband.

Mrs Hinson (*using her "posh" accent*) Who did you say he was again?

Roma Ginger Rogers.

Mrs Hinson (*to Michael*) Far be it from me, dear—but Ginger Rogers didn't have a moustache. Not in *The Barclays Of Broadway* she didn't. And her hair was longer.

Michael (*with gritted teeth*) I wear—a wig.

Mrs Hinson (*her "posh" accent wearing off*) That's all right, dear—a lot of people do nowadays.

Sandy (*to Jennifer*) What a sweet grey-haired old lady. Is she your mother?

Jennifer His mother. Isn't he lucky?

Jennifer goes inside the house

Roma Do sit down, please.

Sandy, who is clearly smitten by Mrs Hinson helps her into a chair

Michael What is she doing here?

David (*to Toby*) What am I going to do with her? (*He picks up a beer*)
Toby I'm starving.
Roma Now then, what can I get you to drink?
Mrs Hinson Well dear, I don't often partake, but when I do, it's generally a
port and lemon.
Roma Oh dear.
Mrs Hinson Don't you worry, Sharon—I'm quite happy sitting here
watching you young people enjoying yourselves.
Sandy *Sweet*. (*To Toby*) Isn't that *sweet*?
Roma (*to David*) Sharon?
David (*whispering to Mrs Hinson*) What are you doing here?
Michael Roma.
Roma Yes, Mickey.
Michael (*hissing; pointing to the bucket*) Look at this.
Roma Oh dear.
Michael Oh dear? Oh *dear*? (*He stalks to the kitchen door*) Roma, I wonder if
I might have a word?

Michael goes into the kitchen

Roma Certainly, darling. (*She turns her hostess smile on the others*) Do excuse
us.

Roma goes into the kitchen following Michael

David (*knocking back his beer*) Well then, off we go, eh, Mum?
Mrs Hinson Don't be so daft, I've only just got here.
Sandy (*bending to "whisper"*) You didn't by any chance notice someone
lurking around outside, did you?
Mrs Hinson Not within earshot, no dear. But I tell you what though—
(*proudly and generally*) my David's executive.
Sandy *Really*. (*She gazes, "impressed" at David*)
Toby What line are you in?
David The greens.
Sandy You're a politician. How *wonderful*.
David No, no—the *greens*. Fruit and veg.
Mrs Hinson My David is the man who introduced the pimento into
Shepherds Bush.
Sandy You're a barrow boy!
David Used to work the market. Now it's three high-class shops and a
delicatessen.
Mrs Hinson I remember the time we couldn't so much as force a carrot down
him, funny how things turn out, isn't it?
Sandy *Fascinating*.

Michael and Roma come out. She is holding a bowl of nuts

Roma As there's a slight hiatus we thought a little nibble to be getting on
with . . .

Toby's face brightens, but turns to disappointment as:

(She proffers the bowl to Mrs Hinson) Mrs Hinson?

Mrs Hinson What are these supposed to be?

David Pistachios.

Roma Do have one.

Mrs Hinson Yes, but what are they?

Michael *(pointedly)* They're a form of nut.

Mrs Hinson Not if they're nuts, no. *(Generally)* The thing is, I've got no mastication. My sister's just the same. Her teeth went immediately prior to her hubby.

Roma Oh dear.

Mrs Hinson She took him a cup of tea and when she went back half an hour later, the tea was stone-cold and so was he. Just sitting there he was, on their uncut moquette settee.

Sandy How tragic.

There is a blast on a van horn

Mrs Hinson struggles out of her chair, aided by the willing Sandy

Mrs Hinson Now then, I'll just avail myself of your toilet before I settle.

Michael Before she what?

Mrs Hinson moves to the french windows with her frame

Roma I'll show you where it is, shall I?

Mrs Hinson Oh I know where it is, thank you. They're all the same, these houses. *(She indicates the french windows)* I tell you what though, Sharon —you want to put a drop of paraffin in the water next time you clean these windows. They come up like new.

Roma They are new.

The Smethurst doorbell rings

Mrs Hinson Door!

Mrs Hinson goes inside, with the frame

Roma More guests!

Toby Great!

Sandy *(whispering)* Gareth!

Michael Hat!

Roma grabs the hat and hurries inside, passing the bowl to the eager Toby who dips hungrily into the nuts and carelessly ejects the shells

David looks over the fence to see where Jennifer is

Michael *(to Sandy; pointing behind her)* Shrub.

Sandy obediently jumps away from the shrub

Michael gives Toby an ashtray for him to put the shells in

David *(conversationally)* My old dad would have a fit if he could see what you've done to this place.

Michael Yes, well, the whole area is improving. And we all know what that
means.
David Yeah, it means that people who should be living here can't afford to
any more.

Sandy clamps a hand over her mouth

Michael Are you a communist by any chance, er, Derek?
David 'Fraid not, Michael—I can only just afford to be a socialist.

Roma hurries out into the garden with her hat still on

Roma Does anyone own the maroon Sierra?
Toby Me.
Roma I wonder if you'd mind moving it?
Toby Again?
Roma Mr McMonagle is having trouble reversing his Dormobile.
Toby Oh—right.

*Toby goes into the house, almost handing someone the bowl, but on second
thoughts deciding to take it with him*

Michael (*shouting after Toby*) Tell him from me I'm getting just about fed up
with this, all right?
David He's always had trouble with that van, old Pat.
Michael He doesn't own the road, you know.
David (*grinning*) I wouldn't tell *him* that.

Michael goes into the kitchen

Roma takes off her hat and dabs at her brow

Roma (*quickly changing the subject*) I expect you're all *starving*. (*She opens
her mouth to continue but sees the nut shells on the paving. She picks them up
and puts them in the bin*) Truth is, we had a slight problem defrosting the
meat. We forgot to take it out of the freezer and our whole schedule has
been—you know—but we'll be eating very very soon, I promise you.

Toby comes out into the garden

Toby Does anyone own the grey Jag?
David Yeah—me.
Toby You'll have to move it before I can move—sorry.

There is another impatient blast on the van horn

David All right, Paddy, all right!

David and Toby go into the house as:

Sandy gets herself a drink

Sandy Lovely party, darling.

*Mrs Hinson comes out through the french windows, pulling down her skirt.
She has left the frame indoors*

Mrs Hinson That's better.

Sandy immediately moves to help Mrs Hinson into her chair

Michael (*calling; off*) Roma!
Roma Coming darling! Do excuse me.

Roma goes into the kitchen as:

Jennifer comes out into the garden

Mrs Hinson Do *you* live local, do you, dear?

Jennifer bends to look through the peephole in the fence

Sandy No, I'm afraid I live in a rather shabby old pile in St John's Wood. At least I did until today.
Mrs Hinson (*sensing gossip*) Oh yes?
Sandy Later—when I know you better. Now then, let me get you a little something.
Mrs Hinson No thank you, dear—I'll just sit here quietly out of everyone's way. I wish I had my *TV Times* though, I could finish reading my article.

Michael comes out of the kitchen

Mrs Hinson I say, Wayne, have you got the *TV Times*—I want to finish reading my article.
Michael (*stiffly*) Sorry, I can offer you *Money Magazine* or *The Lancet*.
Mrs Hinson No thanks all the same, I'm not keen on dancing, never have been to be quite honest.
Michael (*staring at Mrs Hinson*) Roma!

Michael goes into the kitchen

Mrs Hinson My television's broken, you know. It was working perfectly well until You-know-who turned up. I was supposed to be watching my programme at their place.
Sandy *Sweet.*
Mrs Hinson My David's got a twenty six inch.
Sandy You must be very proud.
Mrs Hinson Mind you, he should have—being executive.

Irritated by what she has heard, Jennifer collects the chair and stands on it by the fence

Jennifer (*announcing*) For your information, I didn't touch the rotten television. All right? I didn't touch it. (*She gets down from the chair*)

Jennifer goes inside the house as:

Toby and David come through the french windows as:

Roma comes out of the kitchen with a basket of french bread which she puts on the table

Roma (*brightly*) Not long now, everyone!

Roma goes behind the shed

David (*discreetly*) Time for us to go, Mum.

Toby picks up a piece of bread

Mrs Hinson (*loudly*) I am not going where I am not wanted.

Michael comes out of the kitchen

Roma comes out from behind the shed

Michael He's eating the food.
Roma I expect he's hungry, darling.
Michael Yes, but why is he eating the *food*?
Sandy (*examining the contents of the table*) Bona tuck, Mickey. (*She points*) Oh look—cheese crumble!
Roma We also had trouble defrosting the cheese, I'm afraid.

Roma beams, and goes into the kitchen

Michael (*guiding David to one side*) I say—Derek—(*he makes it sound light*) You—er—you said something about buried treasure. (*He indicates*) Shrub.
David (*avoiding the shrub; confidentially*) There's this story about this strange old spinster lady who lived here once. She had this thing about not trusting banks, her fiance having topped himself during the Wall Street Crash. So she buried all her considerable wealth in the garden in a purpose-built container—just about here, they reckon. (*He points down to the square of earth in which the shrub is planted*)
Michael Oh yes? (*He laughs dryly*)
David Just one of these stories of course, Michael—but there's no smoke without fire as they say. I mean, you take old Mr Holloway down at number twenty-three. He was always going on about this painting he found in the attic and when he dies his son has it valued and it turns out to be this long-lost Van Gogh. Van Gogh! He painted it when he was working over here as assistant to the vicar at Isleworth. So. You never know, do you Michael?

David taps his nose and moves away, leaving Michael staring down at the shrub

The Smethurst doorbell rings

Mrs Hinson Door!

Roma appears in the kitchen doorway

Roma More guests!
Toby Great!
Sandy Gareth!
Michael Hat!

Roma hurries to pick up her hat, then realises she already has it on, and hurries into the house

Michael goes behind the shed

Toby becomes engrossed in helping himself to food, with some difficulty he manages to remove the clingfilm from one of the bowls

Sandy The thing is, d'you see, Gareth says I'm too compliant and not only that, I dress all wrong.

Mrs Hinson And he's a welshman, you say.

Sandy Mostly.

Mrs Hinson (*sucking in air disapprovingly*) Why ever did you marry him?

Sandy I was having a sort of ding-dong with the scrum-half and I suppose I was sort of passed along the line. Gareth plays on the wing, d'you see—there was no-one outside *him*, so he sort of did the decent thing.

Roma comes into the garden with Jennifer

Roma (*brightly*) This is Jennifer—Mr Hinson's wife—she's decided to join us after all.

Mrs Hinson's mouth tightens

Jennifer (*generally*) Hello.

Jennifer takes David's hand

Roma Now then—(*she points towards the shed and the unseen Michael*) this is my husband Michael who's terribly busy at the moment—aren't you, darling!—and this is Sandra Lloyd-Meredith who prefers to be called Sandy and this is Toby Hancock who umm—who umm . . .

Roma averts her eyes from Toby who is eating with his fingers

Everyone else you know, of course. What can I offer you to drink?

Roma takes off her hat and guides Jennifer to the drinks table

Jennifer Oh, a white wine, I think.

Roma Super. (*She pours the wine*) Your husband mentioned that you've just come out of hospital—nothing serious I hope?

Mrs Hinson (*to Sandy*) She's supposed to be internal but we could all say that, couldn't we?

Jennifer No—nothing serious. They think I'm being slowly poisoned.

Roma Oh dear, something in your system?

Jennifer No—something in my family.

There is a blast on a horn

Michael (*calling; off*) Roma!

Roma Coming darling! Excuse me.

Roma goes behind the shed

Mrs Hinson Suffering isn't a patch on what it was in my day. Now we *did* suffer.

Michael (*off*) I'm just about to put the meat on the barbecue.

Roma (*off*) Jolly good!

Michael (*off*) No it isn't jolly good—how can I commence cooking when I don't know how many I'm cooking *for*?

The others have heard this

Roma comes out from behind the shed and beams at everyone

Roma That's chefs the world over though, isn't it? Terribly temperamental.
Mrs Hinson (*referring to David*) His first wife couldn't cook for toffee. Mind you, she did his shirts beautiful.

The Smethurst doorbell rings

Door!
Roma Off again!
Toby Great!
Sandy Gareth!
Michael (*off*) Hat!

Roma collects her hat and hurries in through the french windows

David moves over to Jennifer at the drinks table

Toby has trouble getting the clingfilm off his fingers and, in order to remove it, drapes it over the trellis:

Mrs Hinson He sounds like an animal, your Gareth.
Sandy Darling, the stories I could tell *you*.
Mrs Hinson And you've got nowhere to live?
Sandy Nowhere.
Mrs Hinson (*beckoning her closer*) Only the thing is you see, Sandra—I shall be going to stay with my son for a few months so if you fancy you could make use of my place while you sort yourself out.
Sandy How incredibly generous.
Mrs Hinson Pop round and have a look at it. (*She looks for her doorkey in her handbag*)
Sandy (*doubtfully*) Well . . .
Mrs Hinson Actually, I shall be moving in with my son permanent sooner or later, so my place will be on the market if you're interested.
Sandy (*suddenly very interested*) Really?

Michael comes out from behind the shed as:

Roma hurries out into the garden

Roma I'm terribly sorry but—(*she sees the clingfilm sticking to the trellis and averts her eyes*) would you mind moving your car again—Mr McMonagle has come back and there's nowhere for him to unload his van.
David Which one?
Roma Ummm . . .

David goes into the house, followed by Toby as:

Michael comes out from behind the shed

Roma tries to hide the clingfilmed trellis from him

Michael Not that bloody Irishman again?
Roma Mr McMonagle, yes, Mickey.
Michael Look, go and tell him that's it—no more. He can bloody well park somewhere else—he's not having *my* space.
Roma Mickey, you know how I hate confrontation.
Michael Just remind him that I happen to be a doctor and liable to be called out at a moment's notice, day or night.

Michael goes behind the shed

Mrs Hinson stands staring

Mrs Hinson (*instantly alert*) Doctor? Who's a doctor?
Roma My husband. (*She picks the clingfilm off the trellis*)

Roma goes through the french windows, taking the clingfilm with her

Mrs Hinson (*in total awe*) He's a doctor.
Jennifer Oh god.
Sandy Funnily enough, he's a rather good one, actually.

Michael comes out from behind the shed and shouts through the french windows

Michael You might also ask him when he's going to shift that bloody stupid caravan!
Mrs Hinson Doesn't he speak beautiful? (*To Michael*) I think doctors are wonderful.

David comes into the garden

David I'm all right, it's the other one.
Jennifer You told me he was a milkman. (*She moves near the shrub*)

Michael moves to the table to inspect the food

Mrs Hinson (*tugging at his frock*) Do you know Doctor Stein?
Michael No.
Mrs Hinson He did my veins.
Michael (*to Jennifer*) Shrub! (*He indicates the shrub that Jennifer is near*) Thankyousomuch.

Michael goes behind the shed as:

Roma comes out into the garden

Roma (*excessively bright*) There now, is everyone happy? (*To Jennifer*) Let me freshen your drink.
Mrs Hinson Yes, I would—before she gets withdrawal symptoms and starts breaking the furniture.

Roma moves to replenish Jennifer's glass

David Come on, Mum, time for us to go.

Mrs Hinson I am not going where I am not wanted.
Jennifer (*toasting Mrs Hinson*) Happy families!

Toby comes out into the garden as:

Michael comes out from behind the shed

Michael Roma, I shall now start serving.
Roma Lovely!
Michael And I should like to point out that, as things stand at the moment, each guest will be receiving five pork chops and seven sausages. Where are all your friends?

Michael glares at her and goes behind the shed

Roma looks around hopelessly. Suddenly she is galvanised into action. She seizes up a pile of paper plates and moves round, thrusting a plate at everyone

Roma (*suddenly shouting*) Food everybody! Food! Fox, oboe, oboe, dog! Food! Food, food, food! Food, food, food, food, food!
Michael (*off*) Roma!

Roma dutifully hurries behind the shed

Toby (*speaking quietly to Sandy*) You wouldn't rather pop off somewhere for a spot of dinner *à deux* by any chance?
Sandy Sounds delish, but not tonight, cherub.
Toby Oh.
Sandy Tell you what though—(*she crooks a finger*) follow me.

Sandy goes in through the french windows

Toby looks around and discreetly goes in after her pinching a bottle of wine on the way

Jennifer (*calling towards shed*) Lovely food!
Mrs Hinson (*poking at the food on the table*) I don't like the look of it myself. I mean—where's the nourishment?
Jennifer (*hissing at Mrs Hinson*) We're eating at home.
David Yes, come on, Mum.
Mrs Hinson Come on Mum, come on Mum, that's all I ever get—come on Mum.
David We're going *home.*
Mrs Hinson I'm not having you drive all that way without some food in your stomach. I wonder if she's washed this lettuce?

Roma comes out, beaming, with a plateful of over-barbecued sausages

Roma Jolly good. (*She realises Toby and Sandra aren't there*) Everyone! (*She puts the plate on the table*) Plenty more where this came from! (*To Mrs Hinson*) Do help yourself.
Mrs Hinson Oh no, Sharon, no—I'm not eating off cardboard. (*To David, taking his plate*) Don't you touch anything until I've got you a decent plate

Mrs Hinson goes into the kitchen

Roma takes up a sausage and stares at it as:

Michael comes out from behind the shed, mopping his brow

Michael Roma, you're nibbling!
Roma No Mickey, I'm eating. (*She takes a large bite of sausage*)

Michael goes behind the shed and then goes into the kitchen

Sandy discreetly enters the Hinson garden, followed by Toby. At her instigation, they talk in whispers and discreetly peep over the fence as:

Toby Yes, of course I enjoy your company but I don't *quite* understand what we're doing here. (*He takes a swig from the bottle*)
Sandy That sweet grey-haired old lady has just told me she's about to put it on the market.
Toby Ah yes of course—you're an estate agent!
Sandy Property consultant actually. You know, darling—(*she touches his lips*) premises, premises.
Toby She wants you to negotiate the sale.
Sandy (*with a finger to her own lips*) She will do, cherub, she will do. Now you be a clever little pixie and keep your ears open while I have a wander round to see what's on offer.

Sandy blows him a kiss and goes into the Hinson house

During the following, Toby dutifully listens at the fence, but then he gets fed up and wanders into the shed, knocking back the wine

Roma moves from Jennifer to David who is getting himself another beer

Roma Your wife tells me you're going to Spain in September.
David Yeah, we're very fond of Spain.
Roma *Habla espanol?*
David Sorry?
Roma *Habla espanol?* (*She enunciates, as though to a foreigner*) Do you speak Spanish?
David Oh, *hablo espanol? Claro, que hablo espanol, hombre. En mi opinion el hecho de que puedo tener una conversacion con los espanoles muestra que tengo un respeto profundo por ellos. Bien?*
Roma (*beaming*) Quite. (*She puts David's discarded pull-ring into the bin*)

Michael comes out of the kitchen and takes Roma to one side

Michael Roma, that woman is wandering around our house.
Roma (*with her fixed "hostess" smile*) I don't see that she can be doing any harm.
Michael She's going through the *cupboards.* And where's thingy and whatsit?
Roma (*maintaining her "hostess" smile*) I don't know, Michael—I don't know.
Michael Keep them all *together.*

Mrs Hinson comes out with some china plates

Mrs Hinson Ah there you are, Doctor. I was wondering if you could give me a prescription while I'm here?
Michael What for?
Mrs Hinson Oh I don't mind, really—how about something for my nerves?
Michael Who *are* you?
Jennifer My mother-in-law. Isn't she sweet?
Roma *Sweet.*
Mrs Hinson The thing is, I get very breathless when I run.
Michael So do I.

Michael goes behind the shed

Mrs Hinson (*to Roma; undeterred*) He's not giving much away, is he? I suppose he's private. Now then, food. (*She pokes at the food on the table*)
David Look, we've had our drink, will you please come home?
Mrs Hinson I am not going where I am not wanted.
Jennifer We don't *know* these people.
Mrs Hinson Well you should do—he's a doctor. And between you and me, by the way she dresses, I wouldn't be surprised if she wasn't a Justice Of The Peace. Like that Mrs Curzon who kept the fish shop. Why do you think I'm being so nice to them? I'm trying to do you a bit of good, my son. Now then. Let's see if I can find you a decent bit of meat . . .

Michael comes from behind the shed

Mrs Hinson I say, Wayne, where are your kiddies?
Michael Wayne? What does she mean—Wayne?
David I think she means red wayne or white wayne.
Mrs Hinson Your *twins.*
Roma They're staying with my mother.
Jennifer Twins? That's clever of you.
Roma Just a question of pushing twice as hard, really. But then, as Mickey says—don't you, darling?—you don't get anywhere in this world without pushing.
Mrs Hinson (*pulling Michael's frock*) I say, *she* can't have children.

Michael, David, Roma and Jennifer stare at her

Michael Who?
Mrs Hinson You-know-who. (*She indicates Jennifer*)

David, Michael and Roma's eyes turn from her to Jennifer

Jennifer (*generally*) We don't want children. Sorry.
Mrs Hinson His previous could have children.
Roma Rosemary, you mean?
David Oh my god.
Mrs Hinson Just a mo, I've got my snaps here somewhere.

Mrs Hinson digs into her bag, but David moves to stop her

David Not now, Mum, eh?

An escalating struggle ensues with Mrs Hinson trying to get her bag open and David trying to keep it shut, with Michael, Roma and Jennifer watching

Mrs Hinson I want to show them—my—snaps!
David Not—now!

Mrs Hinson traps his hand in her bag. He barely manages to stifle his cry of pain and smiles round at the others who have watched the struggle

Michael goes to the kitchen door

Michael Roma, I wonder if I might possibly have a moment?
Roma Certainly darling. Do excuse us.

Roma beams her "hostess" smile and goes past Michael into the kitchen. Michael follows her and closes the door behind them

The Light slowly begins to fade

David What are we going to do?
Jennifer I know what *I'm* going to do. I'm going to tart myself up, go out, and give myself to the first man who can prove he's an orphan. (*She moves to the french windows*) I'm going home to get drunk, and so should you.
Mrs Hinson Jump to it, boy—madam has spoken.
David (*decisively to Mrs Hinson*) Right, say good-night and thank them for the drink. (*To Jennifer*) That's it, we're off.

David takes Jennifer's arm and guides her in through the french windows

Mrs Hinson sits po-faced, looking straight ahead, as:

Toby backs out of the Hinson shed and turns. Under the fez he now wears the gasmask. He drunkenly goes into what he believes to be a hilarious version of the Hunchback of Notre Dame. He moves across, with limited vision, dragging his leg, and bumps into the chair, then climbs up on it so that he can "pose" grotesquely over the fence

Mrs Hinson ignores him

So he begins making noises behind the mask

Mrs Hinson still ignores him

Toby gets down from the chair as:

Sandy puts her head out of Mrs Hinson's frosted bathroom window

Sandy Psst!

Toby turns to look round the garden

Up here!

Toby looks up at her, automatically stepping backwards as he does so. He stumbles heavily into the pond as:

Sandy indicates for him to keep his voice down

Darling, I'm trapped! In the loo—the lock's stuck! For god's sake rescue me, I can't stand this wallpaper!

Sandy goes out of sight

Toby gets out of the pond and falls back in again. He hauls himself out and stares down at his shoes and trouser bottoms which are soaked and stained

Toby goes into the Hinson kitchen, squelching as he goes as:

Michael comes out of the kitchen, followed by Roma. He goes straight behind the shed, ignoring Mrs Hinson

Roma Sorry about that. Well now, is everybody happy? (*Her face drops when she sees that only Mrs Hinson is present. She looks around desperately*) Where is everyone?

Mrs Hinson Oh don't worry about them, Sharon—I was about to show you my snaps.

Roma Yes, yes, you were, weren't you? (*She beams graciously but then suddenly, wildly*) Music! How stupid, we've forgotten the music! And the lights! Where are the lights!

Roma hurries into the kitchen as:

Mrs Hinson Well that's charming, I must say. (*Shouting*) I say that's charming that is I must say!

The fairy lights come on and suddenly the music thunders out. The following is performed as a mime sequence

Roma dances away out of the kitchen as:

Michael comes, protesting, from behind the shed

Roma takes him in her arms and dances with him wildly, despite his protestations . . . .

Sandy opens the window again and shouts for help

Mrs Hinson stands and shouts at Michael and Roma before stomping in through the french windows

David, still wearing the policeman's helmet, comes out into the Hinson garden, followed by Jennifer. He shouts over the wall for his mother to come home as Jennifer shouts for him to leave her

Toby, still wearing the fez and mask but not his shoes, comes out

Toby gesticulates to Jennifer who speaks to David, and they all go inside the house, with David picking up the phone on the way

The music stops as suddenly as it started and

Michael and Roma stop dancing as:

Mrs Hinson comes out through the french windows

Michael (*horrified*) You touched my stereo!

Mrs Hinson No, dear, no—I'm not having that, not with my head, not after what I've been through. Now then, who's for a nice cup of tea?

Mrs Hinson goes into the kitchen

Michael and Roma stare after her

Michael (*finally managing*) She touched my stereo!

Michael goes in through the french windows as:

The Smethurst telephone rings

Mrs Hinson puts her head out of the kitchen door

Mrs Hinson Phone!

Roma dutifully hurries in through the french windows

There are the sounds of a car horn and a van horn

Jennifer comes determinedly out of the Hinson house, and goes into the shed, where we hear her banging around as:

Roma, holding the cordless telephone, appears in the french windows as:

Mrs Hinson comes out of the kitchen

Mrs Hinson All I can find is teabags. Haven't you got no proper tea?
Roma It's for you. (*She takes off her hat and drops it on the canvas chair*)

Roma watches, stunned as:

Mrs Hinson takes the telephone and holds it like it's a bomb

There is the sound of car horns and cars crashing

Mrs Hinson Hello? What d'you mean, come home? Who is this?

Jennifer comes out of the shed with a hammer and a large chisel and goes into the Hinson kitchen as:

David comes out of the Hinson french windows, using his mobile telephone. At first he speaks quietly, trying to remain calm

David It's your son and I want you to come home.
Mrs Hinson How can I come home? I'm just gonna make them a nice cup of tea . . .

There is violent knocking at the Smethurst door

Mrs Hinson Door!

Roma comes out of her trance and hurries inside

There is the sound of violent hammer blows from inside Mrs Hinson's house

David stands on a chair. He stops using the telephone and shouts over the fence

David They don't *want* you to make tea—they don't *want* you poking around in their kitchen—they want you to go home!

There is the sound of ripping timber

> *Sandy opens Mrs Hinson's bathroom window. She is about to scream dramatically until she sees David and Mrs Hinson and thinks better of it. She discreetly closes the window*

Mrs Hinson I am only trying to do my best for people—for all the thanks I get.

> *Michael appears, stunned, in the french windows. He is holding a cassette which trails twisted and broken tape*

Michael (*just about audible*) You touched my stereo.

Roma hurries out of the kitchen

Roma (*seeing Michael*) It's Gareth! He's fighting with the McMonagles! All of them! Do something, Mickey!
Michael (*stunned*) Yes, but she touched my stereo.

> *Michael goes back lifelessly through the french windows*

There is a great crash

> *Roma hurries into the kitchen as several of the fairy lights go on the blink, causing the remaining ones to flash wildly*

David (*trying to remain calm*) Are you coming with us or not?
Mrs Hinson Not after the way she's spoken to me, thankyouverymuch. Your Rosemary would never have spoken to me like that.
David What are you talking about? You hated Rosemary. You've hated every woman who's got within ten yards of me.
Mrs Hinson You're my son. If a mother can't make her own son the occasional rice pudding . . .
David I hate your rice pudding! I hate your custard, I hate your fruitcake, I hate all your food—it's rotten, it always has been—how the old man survived it so long I'll never know.
Mrs Hinson Don't you dare bring your poor dear father into this.
David Poor dear father? Poor dear father? You nagged the life out of him. Why d'you think he spent hour after hour in that stupid bloody shed?
Mrs Hinson I see.

> *Jennifer comes out of the Hinson kitchen. Not without some satisfaction, she holds up the bathroom lock which is still attached to a large lump of the door*

Jennifer All done. I'll wait for you in the car. (*She "smiles" and puts the bathroom lock on the table*)

Jennifer goes into the kitchen

David (*turning to his mother*) You see this—(*he extends the palms of his hands*) nervous exzema. I park my car outside this door and my palms itch and my heart sinks. You're my mother and I love you but I don't like you. I want to—but I don't like you.

There is a moment

Mrs Hinson Don't worry, Son. Don't worry, David. You've said your piece. Still—I shall be dead soon and then I'll be out of your way, won't I? And I'm going to make them a nice cup of tea whether you like it or not. (*She moves briskly towards the kitchen*)

Toby comes out of the french windows, still wearing his lopsided fez, and still sodden from the pond

During the following David gives up and goes into the house

Mrs Hinson passes the cordless phone to Toby on her way into the kitchen

Mrs Hinson You sit down, dear, while I make a nice cup of tea, you look like you could do with it.

Mrs Hinson goes into the kitchen as:

Michael comes out through the french windows and is about to say something to Toby when he sees the wildly-flashing fairy lights

Michael Roma! What's happened to these lights?

Michael goes into the kitchen

There is the sound of a police siren

Toby sits wearily and heavily in the canvas chair—and onto Roma's hat. There is the magnified sound of canvas ripping as the chair collapses inwards—with Toby's behind going right through the canvas seat as:

Michael comes out carrying the steps. He stands on them and fiddles with the fairy lights as:

Sandy comes out through the french windows

Sandy Hello cherubs—has anyone seen my little phonette! Gareth needs to contact his solicitor, d'you see—ah, there it is.

Sandy takes up her phone and is about to go, but becomes aware that Toby is lurching around with the chair stuck to him, like a giant tortoise

You poor darling . . . (*She gets hold of the back of the chair in an attempt to set Toby free*)
Michael Roma!

Roma hurries out and makes to help him but she becomes aware of smoke rising from behind the shed—and the red glow from it

Roma The meat's on fire!

Roma hurries into the kitchen and comes out with a saucepan of water. She goes behind the shed. There is the sound of sizzling water as she pours it onto the barbecue, sending up a cloud of steam as:

Sandy finally levers the chair off Toby who shoots forward and into Michael on the steps

Michael grasps at the plastic downpipe for support. It comes loose in his hand, then the next section/joint comes loose, along with the next piece. Then the guttering comes apart in sections, with each section dangling down by a fixing at one end. At the same time, the lights tangle around his head and shoulders. As Michael tries to free himself water pours down from the gaping upper section of pipe

   Roma comes out from behind the shed. She is smudged with charcoal and is holding the empty saucepan

Michael grabs it from her and tries to catch the water coming down from the upper section of pipe

Toby manages to extricate himself from the chair

Roma picks up her totally-flattened tophat

Roma You've been sitting on my hat. (*She remains staring down at it, stunned*)

   Mrs Hinson comes out of the kitchen with a teapot

Mrs Hinson Now then. Who takes sugar and who abstains? (*She empties the teapot over the precious shrub*)
Michael (*turning to point dramatically*) Out! I want you out of here. All of you—out!
Mrs Hinson (*shouting after them*) Get a grip on yourself, you're a medical man!

   Michael grabs Toby and shoves him and Sandra out of the garden into the kitchen, all the time shouting, "Out! Out!"

   Mrs Hinson bustles into the kitchen

   Roma is left alone, staring down at her ruined hat,

   There is the sound of Mrs Hinson, Sandy and Toby's noisy departure

Michael (*off*) Out! Out!
Mrs Hinson (*off*) Well that's charming, I must say!

The front door slams

There is silence

Roma You've been sitting on my hat. (*Then, quite calmly, she drops the hat*)

   Roma goes in through the french windows, closing them neatly after her but remains behind them

   Michael comes out of the kitchen

Michael Roma?

Michael moves into the garden and sees Roma behind the double-glazed windows

Roma smiles, and then suddenly opens her mouth and gives a huge but silent yell. She continues yelling as:

Michael tries to open the french windows but can't

  Michael hurries in through the kitchen as:

Roma remains silently yelling

  Michael appears in the room

Roma continues to yell as:

Michael quickly pulls the curtains closed

  Mrs Hinson comes out into her garden carrying a bundle

  Toby comes out after her, tucking into a bowl of her custard. He is wearing his white jacket, shirt etc., but now wears a pair of grey flannels that are very wide and too short for him, revealing grey socks and carpet slippers

Mrs Hinson opens up the bundle to reveal it to be Toby's white trousers which she will peg out on the line as:

Mrs Hinson Yes. He's a funny boy, my David. If you ask me, he's on the verge. Well, I'm not surprised, living with You-know-who. I was wondering, Doctor—as a medical man—if you could have a word with him.

Toby Ah well now, not really my province, you see—I'm an anaesthetist.

Mrs Hinson Oh, I think he could do with a good night's sleep.

The Hinson doorbell rings

Mrs Hinson Door!

  Mrs Hinson goes inside, followed by Toby as:

Toby Any more custard, is there?

  Michael comes out of the Smethurst kitchen and goes behind the shed

Roma comes out carrying a sparkler and a lighter. She moves lifelessly DS. *She sits and lights the sparkler*

  Michael comes from behind the shed with a garden spade. He begins to carefully dig the soil around the shrub

Michael Frankly, I'm glad to see the back of them.

Roma Yes.

Michael It was only a courtesy do, anyway. (*He becomes totally engrossed in the digging*)

  Mrs Hinson comes out into her garden

Mrs Hinson (*shouting over the fence*) I say, Sharon, I just answered my front door and would you believe it there's this bloke leaning up against the wall in a coffin. I think he must be for you.

The Smethurst doorbell rings

  Door!

Mrs Hinson bustles back indoors as:

Michael continues to dig . . .

And Roma continues to stare at the sparkler

The Lights fade slowly to Black-out so that only the glow of the sparkler remains as——

the CURTAIN *falls*

FURNITURE AND PROPERTY LIST

GROUND PLAN

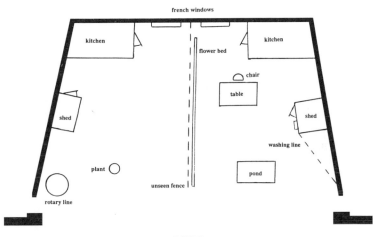

french windows

kitchen

kitchen

flower bed

chair

table

shed

shed

washing line

plant

pond

unseen fence

rotary line

ACT I

On stage: The Hinson's grassed garden

Flowerbeds
Random little piles of plant pots
Plastic bucket
Garden fork
Small pond fashioned from a butler sink sunk into the grass
Old jerry-built shed. *In it:* old-fashioned deckchair
Washing line
1930s dining chair
Old bamboo table. *On it:* copy of the TV Times
Zimmer walking frame with a basket attached

The Smethurst's paved garden

Old chimney pots. *In them:* trailing plants
New, small shed
Rotary washing line
Pair of hinged trestles
Two table tops
Window boxes. *In them:* colourful plants
Several beds of new shrubs. *In them:* conspicuous labels
Cordless telephone behind the french windows

Off stage: Pair of trestles (**Michael**)
Pile of washing. *In it:* dusters, tea towels, pinafore, underwear (**Mrs Hinson**)
Shopping bags. *In them:* ten french sticks (**Roma**)
Large bag of barbecue charcoal (**Roma**)
Mobile phone (**David**)
Aluminium kitchen steps (**Roma**)
Old-fashioned deck chair (**David**)
Glass of water (**David**)
Screwdriver (**Michael**)
Small pinny, kitchen gloves (**Roma**)
Fourteen pound block of cheddar cheese sealed in plastic. *Written on it in black Pentel:* Cheese-Cheddar (**Michael**)
Two cardboard boxes. *Written on one:* Chops-Lamb. *In it:* chops. *Written on the other:* Sausages-Pork. *In it:* Sausages (**Roma**)
Tea tray. *On it:* teapot, cups, saucers, plate of biscuits (**Mrs Hinson**)
Three tea trays (**Roma**)
Half-eaten biscuit (**Michael**)
Large cardboard package. *In it:* components for a barbecue with a hood, a wheeled tripod stand and an instruction sheet (**Roma** and **Michael**)
Cup of tea (**David**)
Toolbox *In it:* tools (**Michael**)
Bunch of cut flowers (**Jennifer**)
Box. *In it:* shopping provisions (**David**)
Biscuit (**Roma**)
Large club hammer (**Roma**)
Carton of wine (**Michael**)
War-time gas-mask, fretwork pipe rack (**David**)
JBL speaker. *Attached to it:* long piece of wire (**Michael**)
Second JBL speaker (**Michael**)
Tray. *On it:* desert plate, spoon, jug. *In it:* custard (**Mrs Hinson**)
Very large old suitcase (**Mrs Hinson**)
Large hand saw, workmate bench (**Michael**)
Cardboard box. *In it:* shattered chops (**Roma**)
Pieces of chop (**Michael**)

Personal: **Michael:** tissue
Mrs Hinson: damp cloth, handkerchief, handbag. *In it:* bottle of pills
David: good watch, packet of thin cigars, slim gold lighter
Jennifer: handbag. *In it:* packet of cigarettes
Roma: headband

ACT II

Strike: Pair of hinged trestles
Two table tops

On stage: As before
Two tables. *On them:* matching tablecloths. *On one:* various bowls of salads etc. covered with clingfilm. *On the other:* carton of wine, three bottles of lemonade, three bottles of cider, six cans of beer, plastic glasses

Swing-lid bin
Four differing and renovated chairs. *One of them:* canvas with arms
Fairy lights arranged around the trellis

Off stage: Bowl of salad **(Roma)**
Paper plates, serviettes **(Roma)**
Barbecue tool **(Michael)**
Wig, small plastic pinny, yellow kitchen gloves **(Michael)**
Plastic cutlery **(Roma)**
Aluminium kitchen steps **(Roma)**
Small piece of food **(Roma)**
Three different ashtrays **(Roma)**
Ashtray **(Roma)**
Mobile phone **(Sandy)**
Bottle of wine **(Roma)**
Large box of matches **(Michael)**
Broom **(Mrs Hinson)**
Child's plastic policeman's helmet **(Roma)**
Glass of wine **(Sandy)**
Glass of wine **(David)**
Glass of wine, bottle of wine **(Toby)**
Bowl of pistachios **(Roma)**
Plate of over-barbecued chops and sausages **(Roma)**
China plates **(Mrs Hinson)**
Gasmask **(Toby)**
Cordless phone **(Roma)**
Hammer, large chisel **(Jennifer)**
Cassette with broken tape **(Michael)**
Bathroom lock with a large lump of wood attached **(Jennifer)**
Aluminium kitchen steps **(Michael)**
Saucepan. *In it:* Water **(Roma)**
Empty saucepan **(Roma)**
Teapot. *In it:* water **(Mrs Hinson)**
Bowl of custard, spoon **(Toby)**
Toby's white trousers **(Mrs Hinson)**
Spade **(Michael)**
Sparkler, lighter **(Roma)**

Personal: **Toby:** packet of cigarettes, box of matches

LIGHTING PLOT

Property fittings required: fairy lights to be used in Act II
Exterior. The same scene throughout

ACT I

To open: Bright exterior lighting
No cues

ACT II

To open: Early summer's evening exterior lighting. The fairy lights flash dimly

Cue 1	**Michael** goes into kitchen *Cut fairy lights*	(Page 44)
Cue 2	**Michael** follows **Roma** and closes the door behind them *Lights slowly fade*	(Page 73)
Cue 3	**Mrs Hinson:** ". . . I must say!" *Fairy lights come on*	(Page 74)
Cue 4	**Roma** hurries into the kitchen *Several of the fairy lights fuse, causing the remaining ones to flash wildly*	(Page 76)
Cue 5	Smoke rises from the shed *Red light from within the shed*	(Page 77)
Cue 5	There is the sound of sizzling water *Fade red light*	(Page 77)
Cue 7	**Roma** continues to stare at the sparkler *Lights slowly fade to black-out*	(Page 80)

EFFECTS PLOT

ACT I

ACT II

Cue 16	**Roma:** "He's parking the car." *Smethurst doorbell rings*	(Page 45)
Cue 17	**Toby** deposits the match in the ashtray *Smethurst doorbell rings*	(Page 46)
Cue 18	**Sandy** proffers a glass *Irritable blast on a car horn*	(Page 48)
Cue 19	**Michael:** ". . . Where's Gareth?" *Smethurst doorbell rings*	(Page 48)
Cue 20	**Roma** looks at **Sandy** *Smethurst doorbell rings*	(Page 48)
Cue 21	**Roma:** "Mickey, about Gareth . . ." *Sudden blast of music*	(Page 50)
Cue 22	A tug-of-war ensues, the broom becoming a symbol of their relationship *Cut music*	(Page 51)
Cue 23	**Roma:** ". . . it's a party." *Smethurst doorbell rings*	(Page 52)
Cue 24	**Roma:** "Where were we?" *Smethurst doorbell rings*	(Page 53)
Cue 25	**Roma:** ". . . actually." *David's mobile phone rings*	(Page 56)
Cue 26	**Roma:** ". . . that's all—some." *Smethurst doorbell rings*	(Page 60)
Cue 27	**Michael** comes out from behind the shed *Smouldering wig*	(Page 61)
Cue 28	**Sandy:** "How tragic." *Blast from a van horn*	(Page 63)
Cue 29	**Roma:** "They are new." *Smethurst doorbell rings*	(Page 63)
Cue 30	**Toby:** ". . . before I can move—sorry." *Impatient blast on a van horn*	(Page 64)
Cue 31	**Michael** stares down at the shrub *Smethurst doorbell rings*	(Page 66)
Cue 32	**Jennifer:** ". . . something in my family." *Blast from a van horn*	(Page 67)
Cue 33	**Mrs Hinson:** "She did his shirts beautiful." *Smethurst doorbell rings*	(Page 68)
Cue 34	**Mrs Hinson:** "I must say!" *Switch fairy lights on. Music thunders through the speakers*	(Page 74)
Cue 35	**David** picks up the phone on the way *Cut music*	(Page 74)
Cue 36	**Michael** goes in through the french windows *Smethurst telephone rings*	(Page 75)

Cue 37   **Roma** dutifully hurries in through the french windows   (Page 75)
            Car horn and van horn

Cue 38   **Mrs Hinson** takes the telephone   (Page 75)
            Car horns and the sound of cars crashing

Cue 39   **Mrs Hinson:** ". . . a nice cup of tea . . ."   (Page 75)
            Violent knocking at Smethurst door

Cue 40   **Roma** hurries inside   (Page 75)
            Violent hammer blows from inside Mrs Hinson's house

Cue 41   **David:** "—they want you to go home!"   (Page 76)
            Sound of ripping timber

Cue 42   **Michael** goes back lifelessly through the french windows   (Page 76)
            Great crash. Some of the fairy lights go out, others flash wildly

Cue 43   **Michael** goes into the kitchen   (Page 77)
            Police siren

Cue 44   **Toby** sits in the canvas chair   (Page 77)
            Magnified sound of canvas ripping

Cue 45   **Roma** hurries out and makes to help Michael   (Page 77)
            Smoke and a red glow from behind the shed

Cue 46   **Roma** goes behind the shed   (Page 77)
            Sound of sizzling water and a cloud of steam

Cue 47   As **Michael** tries to free himself   (Page 78)
            Water pours down from the gaping upper section of the pipe

Cue 48   **Mrs Hinson:** "I must say!"   (Page 78)
            Front door slams

Cue 49   **Mrs Hinson:** ". . . good night's sleep."   (Page 79)
            Hinson doorbell rings

Cue 50   **Mrs Hinson:** "I think he must be for you."   (Page 79)
            Smethurst doorbell rings

PHOTOSET AND PRINTED IN GREAT BRITAIN BY
THE LONGDUNN PRESS LTD., BRISTOL.